GOD'S FALLIBLE

MAN

A Memoir of a Husband, Father, Son and

Brother

PASTOR ANDRE` JONES

After The Storm Publishing

GO THROUGH TO GET THROUGH... THE STORM

ISBN-13: 978-0692650516
ISBN-10: 0692650512

AFTER THE STORM PUBLISHING, LLC
A Division of Peace in the Storm Publishing, LLC
39 Myrtle Avenue #2
North Plainfield, NJ 07060

Visit our Website at
www.afterthestormpublishing.com

DEDICATION

In loving memory to three of the most amazing women ever: Edrice Thomas, my grandmother; Nanny Clevo Pate, my great-aunt & Billie Jean Jones, my mother. Please rest in heaven knowing your labor with me was not in vain.

ACKNOWLEDGMENTS

To the woman who raised me to believe I could overcome the worst moments of my life, Billie Jean Jones, my mother, I love you to life and know that I will see you one day again in glory.

To my children and grandchildren; I live every day of my life working to be a better man, father and grandfather than I was the day before. I may still have a long way to go, but I thank God for bringing me a mighty long way from who I used to be.

To Nina "Blessy" Wilson-Jones: All I can say is I never would have started this journey if you had not accepted my call, accepted my apology and believed in who I had not yet become. I will always thank God for you.

To Karen Shanell: God knew I needed a best friend and wife who would love and believe rather than judge and doubt. I thank Him for you and for our always and forever.

DISCLAIMER

This book is designed to provide information in regard to the subject matters covered. It is sold and shared with the understanding that the publisher and the author are not engaged in rendering legal, medical or professional services. If such assistance is required, the services of a competent professional should be sought.

The purpose of this book is to provide an informational "view" of a journey to restoration. The author and publisher shall not be liable or responsible for any person or entity with respect to loss or damage caused, or allegedly caused, directly or indirectly, by the information contained in this book.

Winter

I know what to do when a storm is coming; prepare. I know what to do when a storm has passed; recover. But what do I do while I'm in the storm? Hang on…

Day 1

Today I came home from my business trip and my wife and kids were gone! I knew she and her family had talked about her needing space, but to sign a lease for a year???! How am I going to make it for a year without them? We've never been apart that long. I know they are her children, but I've been their father for the last 4 years! Now they're gone just like that? I treated them like they were my own; now nothing?

Okay, what did I do this time? Why can't we just work things out without all the outside influences? We are okay when it is just us. But someone else always has an opinion, a word from the Lord or something else to say about what "we" should do!

Enough about them; what did I do? Was I a Protector, Provider and Priest? Did I even know how to be? Or even that I was supposed to be? Who was my example? How could I see that being raised by my mother and a stepfather who drank, got high, was addicted to porn and beat the hell out of me every chance he got? Great example! I hated him so much that I got into every sport that I could just to be out of the house and not have to deal with him. My sister ended up hanging out with her friends to all hours of the night so she wouldn't have to be home, and my mother worked the night shift and slept all day. That was my example of a "family!" I don't remember ever sitting down to a family dinner or celebrating an anniversary, but I do remember hearing her crying in the middle of the night telling him, "You hit me in my face!"

I grew up very angry and confused. I wanted answers! *I needed answers!* After my mother died a few years later, I started to realize that I may NEVER get the answers I so desired, but that didn't stop me from getting angrier, hurting and from searching!

Over a year ago, I made one of the worst mistakes I have ever made in my life! My wife, who was my fiancée then, and I were in "heated fellowship" over a church banner. I decided it was best for me to leave before things got out of hand. I got in my car and was driving off just as my then fiancée came running out and threw a can of paint at my car. Of course it hit my car... I stopped, jumped out and ran at her as fast as I could. I caught up to her as she got to the side of her truck. My momentum threw us both into the window on the side of her vehicle. *CRASH*! Glass was everywhere. Most importantly, she was cut on her neck, her face, her arm and her back. Blood was everywhere. I was in shock and she was hurt.She grabbed a piece of wood and hit me, screamed and ran inside her apartment. She wouldn't let me in to help. The ambulance came; I left and waited to be arrested at my home. I was not going to fight, argue or deny it. I called her over and over again to see if she was okay, but no one would take my call. No one ever came to arrest or question me. Two things hit me like a ton of bricks as I sat there waiting for the inevitable:

First, the person I loved more than anything was hurt like never before; and second, *I was responsible for it*!

The worst feeling I thought I'd ever feel was knowing that someone I loved was hurt and I couldn't do anything to help them. But FAR WORSE was knowing that I caused the pain! *How could I hurt? <u>This is so stupid</u>! Why did I stop? Why didn't I just keep going? God. Let her be okay!*

I received a call from her the next day and poured my heart out, apologizing to her for me acting like an animal. She agreed to meet at a park so that I could see the damage I had done to the woman that I loved with all my heart. It was <u>*horrible*</u>! I wanted to die, but she said three words that literally saved my life: "*I forgive you.*" How could she? Why would she? She did. I felt like I had been given a billion dollars!

We were married a few months later and on our way to putting that entire horrible mistake behind us for good. So we thought…

I never, *ever* meant to put my hands on her in an unloving way. I didn't just wake up and say, "Let me beat my wife today!" I lost my temper, and instantly hurt as soon as I hurt her. Nothing that she ever said or did justified me doing that! I just did what I saw growing up because I had never dealt with what I had seen growing up! I just lied about what I had seen during my childhood and created in words the kind of life that I wanted people to think I had, but the truth came out when I least expected it!

I AM NOT AN ANIMAL! I DON'T WANT TO LIVE THIS WAY AND I CERTAINLY DON'T WANT TO DIE THIS WAY!

She said she forgave me back then, why leave me now? Why was she giving up on me now? I was ready, willing and able to change! It was still wrong and it *never* should have happened. *EVER!* I hurt the one I loved and it didn't matter what I said or promised; what mattered was what I did. Man! I was planning to spend the rest of my life making it up to her. Now she's gone...

<u>My Help on Day 1</u>

But God showed His great love for us by sending Christ to die for us while we were still sinners. Romans 5:8

<u>Day 2:</u>

I had to call my own sons today to tell them that she left me again. They were not happy. *Do we have a family or not? Do we have little brothers or not? Is she going to still be our mom or not?* I promised them that this would never happen again the last time, I've let them down again. What kind of example am I setting for them? I don't want them to go through anything like this. No divorces, no separations, no abuse, no lies, no adultery and no absentee fathers. Not my boys!

They will not be molested, they will not be abused, they will not be promiscuous; *THEY WILL BE GODLY MEN WITH INTEGRITY*!

In spite of the way I had lived and the mistakes I had made, I have to put a stake in the ground and stop the stuff in me from passing onto them. I have to stop generational curses from manifesting in the lives of my boys, even in the midst of me still dealing with mine. Life isn't going to wait any longer for me to figure it out and death certainly isn't!

Separation and divorce seem so selfish to me right now. They never did before. The only thing that mattered before was for me to be happy. Now what about my boys? All of them! Why didn't I think about their happiness when I was losing my self-control? Why didn't I remember how it felt when I was their age and my mother was packing us up to "start over?" I never wanted to have to explain that to my children ever, and I was doing it again with my oldest! *I let us all down!* This is bigger than my wife and me, and our boys are hurting and confused.

My oldest wants me to just focus on myself now. I have to do it right this time. I can't keep setting a bad example. I told him that I have to try to do it differently than I've ever done it before if I want a different result. Her actions can't dictate my behavior. Just because she no longer wants to be married doesn't give me an out to act like I'm not. The old me would be starting a new relationship already. I'm not the "old me" anymore. Trust me son, there's only one way to do it. I've never gotten it right doing it my way. I'm going to try it His way this time in front of you, *even as it hurts*! I have to be a better example for you, *and I have to do the right thing* because *it's right*! Pray for me son; I need it.

My Help for Day 2

Trust in the Lord with all your heart; do not depend on your own understanding. Seek His will in all you do, and He will direct your paths. – Proverbs 3:5-6

And you husbands must love your wives with the same love Christ showed the church. He gave up His life for her to make her holy and clean, washed by baptism and God's word. – Ephesians 5:25-26

The one who sins is the one who dies. The child will not be punished for the parent's sins, and the parent will not be punished for the child's sins. Righteous people will be rewarded for their own goodness, and wicked people will be punished for their own wickedness."– Ezekiel 18:20

Day 3

Didn't sleep at all. Okay, the truth is, I cried all night long. I'm praying, but I have a problem: how do I ask God to do for me what I wouldn't do for someone else?

I walked out of my first marriage. The only thing she did wrong was trust someone (me) who was not truly ready to let go of the way he used to be. When things didn't go my way, I acted out by blaming her for all of our problems; telling her she wasn't a good wife; she wasn't sensitive to my needs, and ultimately being unfaithful to her.

I wanted her to fix me; to make me the man that I was not man enough to try to become by myself.

I knew she was a good woman and that I had found a good wife in her. I wanted to be a good husband for her, too. What I refused to realize was that I had to deal with my past so that it wouldn't mess up our present and future. I didn't. So when things looked like they were going to go wrong, like everything else had in my life: molested, abused, no affection, told I'd never be anything, abandoned, separated from my family, my mother dying, getting married too young, divorced, losing contact with my child, several meaningless relationships, having a child out of wedlock, no real friendships, and no real relationship with Christ, I would resort to the things that helped ease the pain before I felt it. I'd lie, cheat and steal someone else's heart before I'd get mine broken again. So who suffered the hurt? My last wife.

She wanted to hang in there and I just wanted out. She was willing to make it work no matter what, and I was willing to get out no matter what. She was raised that you didn't get divorced and I grew up having seen very few marriages that lasted. She wanted to go to counseling. I went but was not committed to it. In fact, I walked out when the counselors got too close to the truth about me. She feared the wrath of God if she didn't honor her vows before Him, and I was willing to suffer His wrath to get out of mine. How stupid was I to think I could handle the wrath of God?!

Now I was feeling the wrath of God alright; the wife that I was hopelessly in love with had left me. Now I was willing to do whatever it took and she wasn't. Now I was all in and she wasn't. All I wanted was her and all she wanted was out.

Man! It's probably going to be another one of those nights.

My Help for Day 3

For as he thinks within himself, so he is.: - Proverbs 23:7

Don't be misled — you cannot mock the justice of God. You will always harvest what you plant. Those who live only to satisfy their own sinful nature will harvest decay and death from that sinful nature. But those who live to please the Spirit will harvest everlasting life from the Spirit. So let's not get tired of doing what is good. At just the right time we will reap a harvest of blessing if we don't give up." – Galatians 5:6-9

Day 4

Who can work with all this mess going on? I can't and I have no idea how she can either. This isn't affecting her like it is killing me. I know I have to be able to function. I can't even get started! Now is the time that I'd be ready to move. I could deal with this separation thing *soooo* much better in Florida. That's running, huh?

And then she had the nerve to call me to ask me help her with some stuff over at her new place! I don't want to help you decorate the spot that you got to get away from me! But, I'm not going to be that way. I have to take care of my family no matter where they are. Man! I'm finally getting it and she's gone. It can't be too late!

What's crazy is whatever I was trippin' about doesn't even matter anymore. Why did it then? Why get mad over an un-flushed toilet or the boys' dirty room? Okay, I win; but now I'm alone. Whenever we broke up before, I'd swear that the little stuff wouldn't matter anymore if I had one more chance...I did it again. I get it. I can't control her or anyone else for that matter. My job is to control myself no matter what she does.

I finally realize that the stuff I've been through is nobody else's problem. In fact, why should anyone deal with me and my past? I don't. Why dump something that I hated so much in the lap of those I love the most? How stupid is that?

It's time for me to put it (my past) to rest. It is taking up way too much space in my present and is on its way to my future. I didn't like it back then and I certainly don't like it now!

How do I become who I am and not keep running from who I use to be? How do I stop who I used to be from killing who I'm becoming? God, I could use a little help here!

<u>My Help for Day 4</u>

But Moses told the people, 'Don't be afraid. Just stand still and watch the Lord rescue you today. The Egyptians you see today will never be seen again.'" - Exodus 14:13

People with understanding control their anger; a hot temper shows great foolishness."- Proverbs 14:29

Fools vent their anger, but the wise quietly hold it back."– Proverbs 29:11

But now, O Jacob, listen to the Lord who created you. O Israel, the one who formed you says, "'Do not be afraid, for I have ransomed you. I have called you by name; you are mine.'"– Isaiah 43:1

I knew you before I formed you in your mother's womb. Before you were born I set you apart and appointed you as my prophet to the nations. - Jeremiah 1:5

<u>Day 5</u>

Okay enough about her. Today I start dealing with me!

I'm reminded of the last time we went through separation and faced divorce; I was shown some real truths about ME: I was proud, I was arrogant, I was selfish, I was undelivered, I was fake, I was not healed, I was not true to myself or anyone else, *I FELT AS IF I WAS NOT SAVED!* (The enemy really had my mind here. He wanted me to believe I had done so much wrong that I couldn't be saved. *THE DEVIL IS A LIE!*)

Every time that I found something that proved her infidelities or lies; it got turned right back around to me! *Now you know what it feels like to be lied to. Now you know what it feels like to be cheated on. Now you know what it feels like to be the one who loves someone else more than they love you.*"

The craziest thing of all was that it was not her saying those things to me... It was God letting me see myself! I finally was able to see, feel and understand what I had done to so many others as a result of my pain. So why am I back here again almost exactly one year to the date? Because I buried those things in me and never really let them be killed in me. I covered them up! Then they came back up!

I'm finally in the relationship that I want more than any other and what do you know... the old me (the real me) came too!

God got my attention in a powerful way one night when I was flying in from a business trip while my wife and I were previously separated the year before. It was late and I could see all the lights in the city as we landed. God spoke very quietly to me saying, "Do you see all those light down there?" "Yes," I replied. He then said, "There are over 5 million people down there and you are crying over one of them and it is not Me." *I was crushed*! I realized I was more concerned about the relationship with my wife than I was about my relationship with Him! No wonder things weren't working! I had my priorities out of order! God had not been first in my life...

I then remembered four of the most powerful words that I had ever heard in my life from a very dear friend and the wife of a pastor, "You can start today."

Man! I wish I had gotten started and kept it going back then. But, I can start today.

My Help for Day 5

But if you refuse to serve the LORD, then choose today whom you will serve."– Joshua 24:15

This is what the LORD of Heaven's Armies says: Look at what's happening to you!"-Haggai 1:7

Seek the Kingdom of God above all else, and live righteously, and he will give you everything you need."- Matthew 6:33

You must worship no other gods, for the Lord, whose very name is Jealous, is a God who is jealous about his relationship with you."~ Exodus 34:14

Day 6:

I'm still trying to figure out why I was lied to and set up!

When we went to counseling (at my suggestion) with the counselors that she picked because she didn't trust or respect anyone that I suggested, she told me that all she told them was that we needed counseling on our marriage and that we were referred by a friend of hers. It actually went fine and was coming to a close when the pastor asked the question, "Now which one of you is a pastor?" I looked at my wife in total disbelief, and while I believe in the prophetic, I knew this wasn't it! So I said that I was and the beat down began:

"You have no business being a pastor!"

"You needed to step down and close the doors of the church!"

"How can you handle the affairs of God if your house isn't in order?"

"You needed to focus on saving your marriage, not pastoring."

"You have no Godly character or integrity."

"You are going to send your flock to hell!"

"Did you really feel like you have been called or were you just doing it for the fame and   the money?" (FYI – I never took a salary from the church and paid the rent and musicians myself.)

If this was going to be our "fresh start" and what she "needed" to feel comfortable, then why lie? Why not tell me up front that was what you told them? Why set me up?

Once again, now I know what it feels like.

I wasn't even totally opposed to they're counseling. I just felt like that decision should have been made by my own Pastor and Bishop; not my wife and certainly not them.

Once again, the old me (the real me) has messed up that which meant the most to me. Truth is, it always (has?). I just refused to admit it and accept that "I" killed my witness and testimony in the church, too. I was preaching, but not believing. I was admonishing, but not obeying. I was telling, but not doing. Some got saved, but did I?

My Help for Day 6

You hypocrites! Isaiah was right when he prophesied about you, for he wrote, "These people honor me with their lips, but their hearts are far from me. Their worship is a farce, for they teach man-made ideas as commands from God." - Matthew 15:7-9 (This is for me; not about our counselors.)

For God's gifts and his call can never be withdrawn. - Romans 11:29

It would be better to be thrown into the sea with a millstone hung around your neck than to cause one of these little ones to fall into sin. - Luke 17:2

But Samuel replied, 'What is more pleasing to the LORD: your burnt offerings and sacrifices or your obedience to his voice? Listen! Obedience is better than sacrifice, and submission is better than offering the fat of rams." - 1 Samuel 15:22

This is a trustworthy saying: "If someone aspires to be an elder, he desires an honorable position." So an elder must be a man whose life is above reproach. He must be faithful to his wife. He must exercise self-control, live wisely, and have a good reputation. He must enjoy having guests in his home, and he must be able to teach. Hemust not be a heavy drinker or be violent. He must be gentle, not quarrelsome, and not love money. He must manage his own family well, having children who respect and obey him. For if a man cannot manage his own household, how can he take care of God's church? An elder must not be a new believer, because he might become proud, and the devil would cause him to fall. Also, people outside the church must speak well of him so that he will not be disgraced and fall into the devil's trap. – 1 Timothy 3:1-7

Day 7

I'm not feeling too good about myself. I'm crying and losing sleep over a failing marriage and I have had a failing life for years. I have not been healthy and have infected everyone and everything in my path. So why cry out for a marriage when I need to be crying out for deliverance, for salvation, for a change in me?!

Truth is I'm sick of me. The real me; not who I've pretended to be and became to fit in. I have been lying about who I am since I was 6. That's when I was first violated, and I've been lying ever since.

As I was crying one morning on my way to work, I asked God why I was crying in the voice of a child. He quietly replied, "Did you forget what I showed you before? That was the last time you were honest." I had. She had come back to me that time and I had forgotten all that He had shown me about me, and the truth is, I forgot every promise that I made to Him as well.

I had what (who) I wanted and forgot about Him again. I had my god...her.

Man! This thing is deeper than I thought.

<u>My Help for Day 7</u>

You must not have any other god but me. – Exodus 20:3

He showed you these things so you would know that the LORD is God and there is no other. - Deuteronomy 4:35

But be careful. Don't let your heart be deceived so that you turn away from the LORD and serve and worship other gods. – Deuteronomy 11:16

But in my distress I cried out to the LORD; yes, I cried to my God for help. He heard me from his sanctuary; my cry reached his ears. – 2 Samuel 22:7

Will those who do evil never learn? They eat up my people like bread and wouldn't think of praying to the LORD."– Psalm 14:4

But I will call on God, and the LORD will rescue me."– Psalm 55:16

O Lord, you are so good, so ready to forgive, so full of unfailing love for all who ask for your help. – Psalm 86-5

Day 8

I thought I had put up barriers to never be here again. Not marriage vows, but vows of self-preservation: *I'll never be lonely again! I'll never be divorced again andI'll never let anyone else get too close. No one can see or know the real me. No one will ever accept or forgive or understand me. I will never allow myself to feel pain again. I'll get out before I get hurt again! No one will ever make a fool of me again! I must always fix it. I will never be a fool again!* So much for vows/barriers of protection. They are more like lies to me about myself.

How does someone terminally ill spiritually and relationally fix themselves? How do I perform heart and brain (mind) surgery on myself, especially if I don't trust anyone else?

I've been putting bandages on 36 years of issues. Oh yeah, it hasn't worked and they still hurt!

I accept that I have made my wife my god. I realize that. Now I have to accept that I've tried to be my own god by trying to fix myself. I sure haven't trusted the True and Living God to do it. I've come around Him, but I haven't come to Him; and I definitely haven't given Him all of it or me. So now I react to pain, the possibility of pain, the thoughts of pain, rumors of pain, hints of pain, and don't forget failure…as long as I acted like it and even declared it was going to be okay this time, it would be, right?

It's hard being who you are supposed to be when you're lying about how you really feel.

Now what? All my vows (barriers) for protection are starting to fall…

<u>My Help for Day 8</u>

Give all your worries and cares to God, for he cares about you."– 1 Peter 5:7

O LORD, if you heal me, I will be truly healed; if you save me, I will be truly saved. My praises are for you alone! – Jeremiah 17:14

Worry weighs a person down; an encouraging word cheers a person up."- Psalm 12:25

Don't worry about anything; instead, pray about everything. Tell God what you need, and thank him for all he has done."~ Philippians 4:6

Day 9

A couple of days have passed since my last entry. Just didn't feel like dealing with it, to be honest.

What else could I have done? I stepped down from my church. I joined the church where "our" counselors are the pastors. I sat under "good teaching." I started truly working on my Godly integrity and character. I was told that my heart was now soft and pliable. I repented for all my past and present sins.

I accepted my wife's suggestion that, "a house divided against itself cannot stand," didn't apply to us, and we could work on our marriage even though we were in two separate households.

I continued to pick the boys up, spend time with them, had devotion with them and tried to love all their hurts away as best I could.

I helped her build an entertainment center for her place and actually enjoyed the whole process. We worked fine together and enjoyed each other's company like never before. Best of all, we were patient with each other and accomplished something together.

I washed clothes at her place for the boys almost every day and would never leave a dirty dish in the sink. I wanted her to come home (to her place) to a clean house so all she had to do was relax.

I made sure fresh flowers were there as a sign of our fresh start.

I even refused to argue with her as I had in the past. It wasn't worth it and I wasn't going to let her rude and insensitive comments make me act like the "old" me. I actually surprised myself with that one. Prayer and fasting really works. To God be the glory!

But, none of the above seemed to be enough or she wasn't being totally honest about us working things out and getting back together after her lease was up.

It's actually okay, though. I'm starting to like the new me.

My Help for Day 9

So Jacob worked seven years to pay for Rachel. But his love for her was so strong that it seemed to him but a few days."- Genesis 29:20

Hatred stirs up quarrels, but love makes up for all offenses. - Proverb 10:12

Always be humble and gentle. Be patient with each other, making allowance for each other's faults because of your love."- Ephesians 4:2

Husbands love your wives and never treat them harshly."- Colossians 3:19

But you, Timothy, are a man of God; so run from all these evil things. Pursue righteousness and a godly life, along with faith, love, perseverance, and gentleness."- 1 Timothy 6:11

In the same way, you husbands must give honor to your

wives. Treat your wife with understanding as you live together. She may be weaker than you are, but she is your equal partner in God's gift of new life. Treat her as you should so your prayers will not be hindered.

Finally, all of you should be of one mind. Sympathize with each other. Love each other as brothers and sisters. Be tenderhearted, and keep a humble attitude. Don't repay evil for evil. Don't retaliate with insults when people insult you. Instead, pay them back with a blessing. That is what God has called you to do, and he will bless you for it. For the Scriptures say, "If you want to enjoy life and see many happy days, keep your tongue from speaking evil and your lips from telling lies. Turn away from evil and do good. Search for peace, and work to maintain it." The eyes of the Lord watch over those who do right, and his ears are open to their prayers. But the Lord turns his face against those who do evil.'– 1 Peter 3:7-12

Day 10

Today I gave it ALL up!

I stopped lying to God and myself! I stopped trying to be deep and spiritual and changed my long, drawn out, whining prayer to this:

"Lord, I don't know how to do this, or how it's going to work out, but I will trust You."

That was it. No more, no less. Then the flood gates opened! Lights out, phones off (not on vibrate!), TV off, nobody but God and big 'ole waterhead me!

God began to make it plain to me about me: I was without shape or form and empty, and darkness covered my surface (my life). The Spirit of God was hovering over my surface (my life), but the Spirit wasn't *in* my life! Then God said, "Let there be light, and there was light. (I began to see me.) God saw the light was good to me and separated my light from my darkness (My new life from my old life.) God was making me a new man in His own image. He was not going to build on the old. It had to die. He wasn't going to kill the old me; I had to do it. Time was running out for me to do it. He could restore my marriage in a snap. Do I want my marriage without Him or do I want *Him*?

I was not in the wilderness like the children of Israel eating manna and quail. I was in the Garden of Gethsemane preparing to die to the old me. Everyone that I tried to turn to for answers would be asleep and unable to help me. Everywhere that I tried to run to would become the Garden.

Was I finally ready to say, "Nevertheless, Thy will be done," or was I going to keep whining for another solution, because He was not answering to anything else and would respect my decision. I was going to be talked about, ridiculed and exposed, but unlike Jesus *I was guilty! BUT GOD!* Jesus had already paid the price for what I had done, was doing and will do. All I had to do was crucify my flesh. Forgive them all. *Without* apology or explanation. Say it is finished. Realize that He had never left me or forsaken me. Commit my spirit into His hands.

I said ,"yes," and gave up everything that I had been holding onto for 36 years. No questions asked. My conviction and conversion had begun.

My Help for Day 10

In the beginning God created the heavens and the earth.

The earth was formless and empty, and darkness covered the deep waters. And the Spirit of God was hovering over the surface of the waters.

Then God said, "Let there be light," and there was light.

And God saw that the light was good. Then he separated the light from the darkness. – Genesis 1:1-4

Then God said, "'et us make man in our image, to be like us. They will reign over the fish in the sea, the birds in the sky, the livestock, all the wild animals on the earth, and the small animals that scurry along the ground." 'So God created man in his own image. In the image of God he created them; male and female he created them. Then God blessed them and said, "Be fruitful and multiply. Fill the earth and govern it. Reign over the fish in the sea, the birds in the sky, and all the animals that scurry along the ground.' – Genesis 1:26-28

I am the LORD, the God of all the peoples of the world. Is anything too hard for me?"– Jeremiah 32:27

So Moses and Aaron said to all the people of Israel, "By evening you will realize it was the LORD who brought you out of the land of Egypt." n the morning you will see the glory of the LORD, because he has heard your complaints, which are against him, not against us. What have we done that you should complain about us? ' hen Moses added, "'he LORD will give you meat to eat in the evening and bread to satisfy you in the morning, for he has heard all your complaints against him. What have we done? Yes, your complaints are against the LORD, not against us."' – Exodus 16:6-8

There he told them, "'ray that you will not give in to temptation." ' e walked away, about a stone's throw, and knelt down and prayed, "'Father, if you are willing, please take this cup of suffering away from me. Yet I want your will to be done, not mine." ' hen an angel from heaven appeared and strengthened him. e prayed more fervently, and he was in such agony of spirit that his sweat fell to the ground like great drops of blood. t last he stood up again and returned to the disciples, only to find them asleep, exhausted from grief. "Why are you sleeping?" he asked them. "Get up and pray, so that you will not give in to temptation." - Luke 22:40-46

For I was born a sinner—yes, from the moment my mother conceived me. - Psalm 51:5

Meanwhile, Saul was uttering threats with every breath and was eager to kill the Lord's followers. So he went to the high priest. He requested letters addressed to the synagogues in Damascus, asking for their cooperation in the arrest of any followers of the Way he found there. He wanted to bring them—both men and women—back to Jerusalem in chains. As he was approaching Damascus on this mission, a light from heaven suddenly shone down around him. He fell to the ground and heard a voice saying to him, "'aul! Saul! Why are you persecuting me?" "' 'ho are you, lord?'" Saul asked. And the voice replied, "' am Jesus, the one you are persecuting! Now get up and go into the city, and you will be told what you must do.' - Acts 9:1-6

For God bought you with a high price. So you must honor God with your body."– 1 Corinthians 6:20

Jesus said, "'ather, forgive them, for they don't know what they are doing.' – Luke 23:34

When Jesus had tasted it, he said, 'It is finished!" Then he bowed his head and released his spirit. – John 19:30

Then Jesus shouted, "Father, I entrust my spirit into your hands!" And with those words he breathed is last. – Luke 23:46

Day 11

God is dealing with *me*! God has really done something that has never happened to me in over 36 years...forced me to deal with *my* pain!

I don't like pain; pain has scared me; pain has driven/controlled me... fear of dealing with my pain from molestation, abuse from my step-father, feeling abandoned after the death of my mother and, most recently, my father; feeling pain from failures, divorces, poor choices, hurting others especially those I care about...*I don't like pain*!

I realized that I had to feel and deal with the pain. I can't hide it or from it any longer. That hasn't helped anyway; just hurt more and hurt those I care about. The truth is, I am finally accepting that and not trying to make excuses, blame others or run. I need this and don't want to lose it. I want and need this Gethsemane experience knowing that there is a crucifixion on the other side for me. I have to die to old me and to my pain. I need this Peniel experience knowing that there is a permanent limp (pain) after this struggle, but God will change my name. I am alone with my pain and I need to be!

Here's what God revealed to me about me:

My Help for Day 11

Plans

The Lord brings the counsel of the nations to nothing; He makes the plans of the people of no effect. The counsel of the Lord stands forever. ~ Psalm 33:10-11

I now plan to be available to listen to and do what God tell me to in His Word and destroy my plans! AND I can't be controlled by my pain/fear!

Obedience

But be doers of the Word and not hearers only, deceiving yourselves. ~ James 1:22

I have to just be obedient! Not exceptions or compromise! Not settling for "I'm trying" (afraid of pain), but only the highest level of integrity; *nothing less*! First things first: first I sit, listen and hear, then I learn and go do only what God tells me to do the way _He wants it done_.

Obedience to God will provide the following:
A Godly life

Jesus said, "And I know that His command is everlasting life." ~ John 12:50

The life that is in Him empowers me when I obey.

God's Attention

But on this one will I look: on him who is poor and of a contrite spirit, and who trembles at My Word. ~ Isaiah 66:2

When I am afraid of not living God's Word; at the thought!!! I will never do anything against it. Then I can get excited at the thought of Him doing it through me!!! God loves that so much, He will look down to make sure that I'm blessed!!   !

A Closer Relationship with Him

He who has my commandments and keeps them, it is he who loves Me. And he who loves Me will be loved by My Father, and I will love him and manifest Myself to him. ~ John 14:21

Jesus said obedience is the proof of love, not what I say or pretend to do. Love brings me into a real relationship with God the Father. It also makes others see the image of Christ in me. I will look like Him!!! I will have integrity and Godly character... I will be a credible minister, witness & servant.

An Unshakable Foundation

Therefore whoever hears these sayings of Mine, and does them, I will liken him to a wise man who built his house on the rock; and the rain descended, the floods came, and the winds blew and beat on that house; and it did not fall, for it was founded on the rock. But everyone who hears these sayings of Mine, and does not do them, will be like a foolish man who built his house on the sand; and the rain descended, the floods came, and the winds blew and beat on that house; and it fell. And great was its fall. ~ Matthew 7:24-27

The storms will hit me when I obey Him and when I don't. I am no exception! The question is will I stand? I haven't stood in integrity before and have lost it all!!! I have to die to the old me!!!

Obedience from this day from this day forward will make me ready for any storms that come my way!!! - Oh that you had heeded My commandments! Then your peace would have been like a river, and your righteousness like the waves of the sea... ~ Isaiah 48:18

God is dealing with me!!!

Day 12

I will not have a plan B! God, if you don't fix this situation, it will not get fixed. If You don't save this marriage, it will not be saved. I will not try to find an alternative just "in case" You don't come through. That's crazy! You never fail! Whatever You allow, I will accept. In the name of Jesus. Amen.

My Help for Day 12

Though He slay me, yet will I trust in Him: but I will maintain mine own ways before him. – Job 13:15

The LORD is a shelter for the oppressed, a refuge in times of trouble. – Psalm 9:9

The LORD is good, a strong refuge when trouble comes. He is close to those who trust in him. – Nahum 1:7

Those who live in the shelter of the Most High will find rest in the shadow of the Almighty. This I declare about the LORD: He alone is my refuge, my place of safety; He is my God, and I trust Him. – Psalm 91:1-2

The LORD is my shepherd; I have all that I need. He lets me rest in green meadows; He leads me beside peaceful streams. He renews my strength. He guides me along right paths, bringing honor to His name. Even when I walk through the darkest valley, I will not be afraid, for

You are close beside me. Your rod and Your staff protect and comfort me. – Psalm 23:1-4

Lead me by your truth and teach me, for you are the God who saves me. All day long I put my hope in you. – Psalm 25:5

What shall we say about such wonderful things as these? If God is for us, who can ever be against us? – Romans 8:31

I trust in God, so why should I be afraid? What can mere mortals do to me? - Psalm 56:11

So we can say with confidence, "The LORD is my helper, so I will have no fear. What can mere people do to me?" – Hebrews 13:6

Day 13

I'm reminded of the time, several years ago, when I worked in secular radio and my station sponsored a boat ride party. Two men got into a fight on the boat and made us cut the trip short. As soon as they got off the boat, they started fighting again. Just as I ran up to break them up, the smaller man pulled out a gun and shot the larger man point blank in the chest. I'm standing there as he's now pointing the gun at me yelling, "That's right! I shot him! That's right!" With nowhere to duck or hide, I just dove and rolled as he pulled the trigger. THE GUN DID NOT FIRE! I heard it click several times, but nothing! God didn't save me from that to kill me in this.

I'm reminded of being in college and losing control of the car I was driving in (way too fast I might add). We literally went from one side of the busy street to the other out of control. The car came to a screeching halt in a parking lot… without hitting a thing! God didn't spare me from that to wreck me in this.

I'm reminded of the night that I had an overwhelming feeling that I was going to die soon. I even spoke it to a dear friend of mine who was riding with me at the time. She told me to be careful of what I was saying because it may come to pass. I could not shake it... Hours later a car came careening out of control around a hair pin curve directly at us. All we could do was brace for impact. Tshe car came to a halt right next to us without hitting us! We were driver's side to driver's side and I could see that the driver was drunk. God didn't let that take my life to let it get taken by this.

God has spared me. Why have I tried so hard to kill me?

<u>My Help for Day 13</u>

"For I know the plans I have for you," says the LORD. "They are plans for good and not for disaster, to give you a future and a hope." – Jeremiah 29:11

Nevertheless, I took pity on them and held back from destroying them in the wilderness. – Ezekiel 20:17

For God loved the world so much that he gave his one and only Son, so that everyone who believes in him will not perish but have eternal life. – John 3:16

Day 14

Yesterday God reminded me of the many times He spared my life. Today he reminded me of how He saved my life:

During our separation last year after my wife had filed for divorce, I had a night when I couldn't sleep and couldn't stop crying. I begged God to let me do one or the other; either allow me to cry myself to sleep or be up, but not crying. Either was fine, but Lord please not both! Well He did not relent. Hours passed and I finally cried out, "Who am I to You if I can't get this one thing???" To which He quietly said one word, "Daniel." I have to be honest... I yelled at God, "If I am Daniel then why didn't I see this one coming??? I'm definitely not Daniel!" He didn't say another word.

I finally stopped crying and went to sleep at about 6:30 a.m. only to wake up at 7:30 a.m. with one thing on my mind; get to Compton Memorial Church of God In Christ in Galveston, TX. Why there I had no idea, but I had to get there and there was no other option! I had not been there in years!!!

I first visited there when at the invitation of my ex-wife and a friend to hear Evangelist Joyce Rodgers preach. She had been given a prophetic Word there months before and had heard Joyce speak at a Metamorphosis Conference. They took me there to meet an Elder & his wife, in hopes that my being in the strong presence of the Holy Spirit would wake me up. Evangelist Joyce Rodgers prayed over me prophetically and I were slain in the Spirit. Afterwards, she told me that she saw 'Apostle' written over my spirit. The Elder & his wife adopted me spiritually at dinner that Sunday and have labored over me in the Spirit ever since. Now God was sending me back there. I had no idea what time the service started, but I knew I had to get there late or not! I called and picked up the friend who had invited me previously and we made our way to the church.

Just as we walked in the door, the Elder who had covered me and prayed for me said, "Open your bibles to the book of Daniel." I was through! He began to teach about the "Pride of Nebuchadnezzar" which was the story of my life. I was proud. I was arrogant. I had to make it all about me. I was the victim for their sympathy and the victor for my glory. I had done it all and lied about the rest. God was showing me He had had enough of me!

I was going to be driven from society; I would live in the fields with the wild animals; I was going eat my grass like a cow; I was going to be drenched with the dew of heaven; and I was going to live this way for 7 periods of time until I learned that the Most High rules over the kingdoms of the world and gives them to anyone He chooses.

I ran to altar and fell to my knees and stayed there for the rest of the service apologizing to God for me being me and not who he called me to be!!! I had to accept my punishment; I was guilty. What truly blessed me was the conclusion: The Elder finished the teaching by pointing out that God held the kingdom for Nebuchadnezzar and restored everything to him when he truthfully looked up to heaven and praised and worshiped the Most High! There was even hope for me.

I gave my life to Christ that day, I believe truly for the 1st time. I didn't know how I had gotten off track or even when, but I knew that I was finally pointed in the right direction.

Man! Today was the day that God saved my life through Christ Jesus!

My Help for Day 14

Daniel Explains the Dream

Upon hearing this, Daniel (also known as Belteshazzar) was overcome for a time, frightened by the meaning of the dream. Then the king said to him, "Belteshazzar, don't be alarmed by the dream and what it means." Belteshazzar replied, "I wish the events foreshadowed in this dream would happen to your enemies, my lord, and not to you! The tree you saw was growing very tall and strong, reaching high into the heavens for all the world to see. It had fresh green leaves and was loaded with fruit for all to eat. Wild animals lived in its shade, and birds nested in its branches. That tree, Your Majesty, is you. For you have grown strong and great; your greatness reaches up to heaven, and your rule to the ends of the earth.

Then you saw a messenger, a holy one, coming down from heaven and saying, "Cut down the tree and destroy it. But leave the stump and the roots in the ground, bound with a band of iron and bronze and surrounded by tender grass. Let him be drenched with the dew of heaven. Let him live with the animals of the field for seven periods of time."

"This is what the dream means, Your Majesty, and what the Most High has declared will happen to my lord the king. You will be driven from human society, and you will live in the fields with the wild animals. You will eat grass like a cow, and you will be drenched with the dew of heaven. Seven periods of time will pass while you live this way, until you learn that the Most High rules over the kingdoms of the world and gives them to anyone he chooses. But the stump and roots of the tree were left in the ground. This means that you will receive your kingdom back again when you have learned that heaven rules.

"King Nebuchadnezzar, please accept my advice. Stop sinning and do what is right. Break from your wicked past and be merciful to the poor. Perhaps then you will continue to prosper." ~ Daniel 4:19-27

The Dream's Fulfillment

But all these things did happen to King Nebuchadnezzar. Twelve months later he was taking a walk on the flat roof of the royal palace in Babylon. As he looked out across the city, he said, "Look at this great city of Babylon! By my own mighty power, I have built this beautiful city as my royal residence to display my majestic splendor."

While these words were still in his mouth, a voice called down from heaven, "O King Nebuchadnezzar, this message is for you! You are no longer ruler of this kingdom. You will be driven from human society. You will live in the fields with the wild animals, and you will eat grass like a cow. Seven periods of time will pass while you live this way, until you learn that the Most High rules over the kingdoms of the world and gives them to anyone he chooses."

That same hour the judgment was fulfilled, and Nebuchadnezzar was driven from human society. He ate grass like a cow, and he was drenched with the dew of heaven. He lived this way until his hair was as long as eagles' feathers and his nails were like birds' claws. ~ Daniel 4:28-33

<u>Nebuchadnezzar Praises God</u>

After this time had passed, I, Nebuchadnezzar, looked up to heaven. My sanity returned, and I praised and worshiped the Most High and honored the one who lives forever.

His rule is everlasting, and his kingdom is eternal. All the people of the earth are nothing compared to him. He does as he pleases among the angels of heaven and among the people of the earth. No one can stop him or say to him, "What do you mean by doing these things?"

When my sanity returned to me, so did my honor and glory and kingdom. My advisers and nobles sought me out, and I was restored as head of my kingdom, with even greater honor than before.

Now I, Nebuchadnezzar, praise and glorify and honor the King of heaven. All his acts are just and true, and he is able to humble the proud. ~ Daniel 4:34-37

Day 15

Now that it was fresh in my mind how God spared me and saved, the work had to begin.

I had to go back and make some things right.

Too many people had been hurt by me for no other reason than the fact I did not want to deal with my past hurts. I was literally like a cancer who had infected every "cell" (person who tried to give me life) that I had come in contact with. I killed all of their hopes and all of their dreams of a life with the man they thought I was. Not only did I kill their hopes and dreams, but those of their mothers, fathers, sisters, brothers, friends and families whom they (AND I) convinced that I was the one who would take care of their loved one.

I didn't! God was not going to let me off the hook that easy. While I was forgiven, there were still consequences for my actions. If I had robbed a bank and gave the money back, I'd be forgiven, but I'd still be on my way to jail.

Man! I have to make some calls...

<u>My Help for Day 15</u>

Confess your sins to each other and pray for each other so that you may be healed. ~ James 5:16

When you become aware of your guilt in any of these ways, you must confess your sin. ~ Leviticus 5:5

Day 16

Call number one: My wife who I walked out on because I felt like I had made a mistake by marrying and was tired of being married to. Man! I just knew she was going to curse me out! It has been years...

God why do I have to start with her? I had to start with the worst of the worst to be able to start to get back to His best. But she didn't betray me, I betrayed her! She was the one who didn't return evil for evil to me! The one who stood on the Word and honored our vows when I didn't! I had to learn how to finally obey Him in spite of my issues, fears, emotions, wants and wishes AND she had been a living example of that whether I was ever ready to admit it or not.

These were the hardest 10 digits I had ever dialed in my life, but God is not playing with me anymore. I felt like my life would end if I didn't do exactly what He told me to do at that very moment without exception or excuse! She took my call and didn't hang up. I didn't waste any time and just began to apologize for all the hurt, all the pain, all the wrong that I had caused her. I told her that she had done nothing wrong except trying to love someone who truthfully didn't love himself.

I had not been honest with her about who and where I really was. I even confessed my affairs and other stuff not previously revealed. I had to get it all out! It was killing me and had killed her too. She didn't deserve any of it and I gave it all! She forgave me that night and has been one of my best friends here on earth ever since. God is amazing!

Even crazier than her forgiving me and becoming a true friend...she began to help me deal with my separation and pending divorce! Not with ulterior motives, but with the Word of God and her testimonies from having dealt with me! God is amazing! I poured out my heart to her about my wife and tearfully longed for my wife and our marriage.

I continued to answer all of the unanswered questions about the demise of the relationship between my ex-wife and I that God hadn't provided for her when she went through this recovery & healing process. Clearly God's delivering her from the pain I caused her enabled her to listen to me go on and on and on and on and on and on (and cry uncontrollable) for another woman and still minister to me for my own deliverance.

She had pledged to be my 'sheepdog' as I shepherded my flock when I was ordained. Though our marital vows were broken, she honored our spiritual vows for ministry in faith even while I was lost.

I thank God because not many ex-wives get the opportunity to get the answers that He gave her especially when they had been hurt so badly. Then to turn around and minister to me through the same thing??? I don't know if I would not have said, "That's good for you!" under my breath while I was listening if the roles had been reversed. Just being honest... I thank God that she handled me according to His Word and will. She was the one who listened to the prophetic Word that said she would stand beside me through my storms and accepted the Word even when I rebuked it. I married her, but once again I didn't trust my heart with her. I didn't trust her with the truth about me and I couldn't keep being fake with someone who was real in Christ and true to His Word. She was a good woman and I didn't know who or what I was! I didn't believe in her then, let alone trust in who God said she was to me then, "flesh of my flesh and bone of my bone." I had to now. God was sending me back to do now what I didn't do back then.

I had made a vows before Him and I had to keep them one way or another; with or without the marriage to her! She did what He called her to do as a wife in spite of me; now I had to learn how to do what He called me to do as a husband in spite of me. God did all of this on a Sunday morning. He was starting me on a new life in Him; a resurrection.

GOD IS AMAZING!!! And this is call number 1.

My Help for Day 16

So if you are presenting a sacrifice at the altar in the Temple and you suddenly remember that someone has something against you, leave your sacrifice there at the altar. Go and be reconciled to that person. Then come and offer your sacrifice to God. ~ Matthew 5:23-24

You have heard the law that says, "Love your neighbor' and hate your enemy. But I say, love your enemies! Pray for those who persecute you! In that way, you will be acting as true children of your Father in heaven. For he gives his sunlight to both the evil and the good, and he sends rain on the just and the unjust alike. If you love only those who love you, what reward is there for that? Even corrupt tax collectors do that much. If you are kind only to your friends, how are you different from anyone else? Even pagans do that. But you are to be perfect, even as your Father in heaven is perfect." ~ Matthew 5:43-48

And they have defeated him by the blood of the Lamb and by their testimony. And they did not love their lives so much that they were afraid to die. ~ Revelation 12:11

If you forgive those who sin against you, your heavenly Father will forgive you. But if you refuse to forgive others, your Father will not forgive your sins. ~ Matthew 6:14-15

Do not judge others, and you will not be judged. Do not condemn others, or it will all come back against you. Forgive others, and you will be forgiven. ~ Luke 6:37

So watch yourselves! "If another believer sins, rebuke that person; then if there is repentance, forgive. Even if that person wrongs you seven times a day and each time turns again and asks forgiveness, you must forgive." ~ Luke 17:3-4

Day 17

The difficult thing is while God is taking me through this process, life is still happening. My wife is starting a new "friendship" at her job. Every word out her mouth is either this person's name or something that they said. She even cuts conversations off with me to start talking about this person again. I can tell that I'm irritating her, but I can tell that this person intrigues her very spirit.

Even though we are apart, I have to do what I'm supposed to do as her husband. I can't keep doing it wrong and expecting it to turn out right. I can't let her behavior dictate mine. I could no longer call myself a husband; I had to be one; but how? According to God's Word!

Every time that my wife brought this person up I began to tell her how much I thanked God that He had brought her someone she could relate with on her job. I told her to tell this person that I thanked God for them being the answer to my prayers for my wife to have some fellow-believers on her job. Now she had another believer that she could be in agreement with and God would be in the midst. I began to speak life into what could have easily been a deadly issue to our marriage. If it was the beginning of the end, I was not going to add fuel to the fire.

Now I could see my opportunity and need to be the priest, protector and provider for my marriage. Normally I would have been overcome by my emotions and anger, but I could no longer lose control of my temper and impale my marriage.

My wife actually became very short, impatient and even rude to me on several occasions, but I refused to react. I would literally be giving her an excuse to dive head first into her new "friendship," and I was not going to further sabotage this marriage. My arguments with her ceased and I began to "argue" with myself about not letting her behavior affect mine. "Why is that upsetting to you?" "Why does that bother you?" "DO NOT

RESPOND!" "This is not your battle!" These are the conversations that I began to have internally and bless God; they began to affect my external behavior!

God was truly helping me control my anger and myself! Even though my wife rarely acknowledged it; I knew a change was taking place and God was pleased! Maybe I wasn't the "new friend," but I was becoming a new man!

My Help for Day 17

A gentle answer deflects anger, but harsh words make tempers flare. ~ Proverbs 15:1

Don't say, "I will get even for this wrong." Wait for the LORD to handle the matter. ~ Proverbs 20:22

Never pay back evil with more evil. Do things in such a way that everyone can see you are honorable. ~ Romans 12:17

Don't repay evil for evil. Don't retaliate with insults when people insult you. Instead, pay them back with a blessing. That is what God has called you to do, and he will bless you for it. ~ 1 Peter 3:9

This means that anyone who belongs to Christ has become a new person. The old life is gone; a new life has begun! ~ 2 Corinthians 5:17

Husbands love your wives and do not be bitter toward them. ~ Colossians 3:19

Who gives life to the dead and speaks of the nonexistent things that [He has foretold and promised] as if they [already] existed. ~ Romans 4:17b

Day 18

My wife has to get up extremely early to get to her job every morning for the next 3 weeks. It is in my heart to get up with her to cover her in prayer and at least be with her on the phone so that I know she makes it into her job safely while it is still dark outside. I am noticing that she is not only getting other calls at no-o'clock in the morning, but she is also getting off with me to take them. I would normally lose my temper, but I refuse to let this behavior get to me. I am going to do what I am supposed to do.

I remember the words one of the best brothers God has ever allowed me to meet shared with me when my wife had filed for divorce, "I went through two years of this so you wouldn't have to go through one!"

He shared a vision that the Lord had given him of his wife drowning in the deep end of a pool. There were people in the shallow end, the middle and the deep end, but his wife was still drowning. He jumped in to swim to her rescue, but every time he tried to save her, she pulled him under and almost caused him to drown. He kept telling her, "Stop fighting me. I'm trying to save you!" She kept pulling him under. He finally swam to the side and saw Jesus. He asked Jesus why she wouldn't stop fighting and let him save her? To the Lord replied, "She's not yours to save. She, like everyone else in this pool, should be floating." That's faith. That's trusting God with even the ones we love the most. That's not easy! Especially when we see those we care about doing things that we know will hurt them!

Then my friend began to tell me to just float and trust God with my marriage. God would take care of her if she just began to "float," but what He really wanted was me! He was literally looking for me like He looked for Adam in the Garden of Eden after he and his wife committed the first sin, "Adam, where are you?" My brother in Christ told me that God was looking for me to finally have the relationship with me that He had planned for me before I was born. Even though I had gotten way off track, He wanted me more than I could imagine and all I had to do was stop focusing on her and put all my attention, desires, and hopes in Him.

He and another brother prayed with me. We encouraged each other. We believed in each other. We checked on each other and we held each other up. Never once did we condemn one another; even if one of us (usually me) got "off the boat." That meant someone stopped floating and jumped back into the mess with our wives. We had to trust God with all our hearts, minds and souls and accept whatever He allowed; not what we made happen! Most of all, we gave God all the glory! We never bashed our wives or spoke ill of them. In fact we prayed for marriages all over, and believed Him for ours.

Man! I finally had an example of Godly men after God's own heart! God had not forgotten me in my sins and mistakes. He sent me the help that I needed and reminded me that I still had it.

My Help for Day 18

So now that you know God (or should I say, now that God knows you), why do you want to go back again and become slaves once more to the weak and useless spiritual principles of this world? ~ Galatians 4:9

God's way is perfect. All the LORD's promises prove true. He is a shield for all who look to him for protection. ~ 2 Samuel 22:31

Offer the sacrifices of righteousness, and trust in the LORD. ~ Psalm 4:5

Those who know your name trust in you, for you, O LORD, do not abandon those who search for you. ~ Psalm 9:10

God is our refuge and strength, always ready to help in times of trouble. ~ Psalm 46:1

But the Lord God called to Adam and said to him, "Where are you?" ~ Genesis 3:9

A person standing alone can be attacked and defeated, but two can stand back-to-back and conquer. Three are even better, for a triple-braided cord is not easily broken. ~ Ecclesiastes 4:12-13

May he send you help from his sanctuary and strengthen you from Jerusalem. ~ Psalm 20:2

But when the Father sends the Advocate as my representative—that is, the Holy Spirit—he will teach you everything and will remind you of everything I have told you. ~ John 14:26

Day 19

What I'm finding is it is easier to deal with my situation when I get up even earlier than my wife and start my day in God's Word, in His secret place and in prayer. I have not gotten the least bit angry at her being very short with me, impatient and rude. It is becoming clearer every day that this is not about her; it is about the changes He is making in me.

I have called every "ex" I could find: ex-wives, ex-girlfriends, ex-friends with benefits, ex-people that I "had to put in check," ex-anyone that I had acted unbecomingly in any way, shape, size or fashion.

Not every one of those conversations was well-received or pleasant. Not everyone was blessed to get my call. God told me to keep calling. I wasn't doing it for reactions, I was being obedient. My first wife said that I had freed her from stuff that she had carried for almost 20 years. To God be the glory. I had no idea. Several people asked, "Why now?" I couldn't leave this life, existence, and place in time with an unrepentant heart. Even if they didn't accept it, I had to confess and ask for forgiveness. Many began to confess their own issues. God got the glory.

I called my oldest son and told him that I was sorry for being a poor example of a father, a husband and a man. I apologized for every time that I failed him by the way that I chose to live my life in front of him. I had the opportunity to raise him from the ages of 6-16. I had made plenty of willful mistakes and I had to confess and apologize to him. I then told him I didn't want him making the same mistakes I made nor did I want him mistreating women the way I had. I talked to him about being upfront and honest no matter what the situation was. I also talked to him about the importance of keeping himself under control, and NEVER put his hands on a woman!

He received every word and shared with me some of the hurt I caused him. He forgave me after sharing his true feelings and express how that conversation freed him from things he had been carrying. To God be all the glory!!! He even start making some calls of his own to his "ex's". I think I could feel God smiling.

My Help for Day 19

But whenever they were in trouble and turned to the LORD, the God of Israel, and sought Him out, they found Him. ~ 2 Chronicles 15:4

All in Judah were happy about this covenant, for they had entered into it with all their heart. They earnestly sought after God, and they found Him. And the LORD gave them rest from their enemies on every side. ~ 2 Chronicles 15:15

But from there you will seek the LORD your God, and you will find Him if you search for Him with all your heart and all your soul. ~ Deuteronomy 4:29

But at the evening offering I arose from my humiliation, even with my garment and my robe torn, and I fell on my knees and stretched out my hands to the LORD my God; and I said, "O my God, I am ashamed and embarrassed to lift up my face to You, my God, for our iniquities have risen above our heads and our guilt has grown even to the heavens. ~ Ezra 9:5-6

They remained standing in place for three hours[a] while the Book of the Law of the LORD their God was read aloud to them. Then for three more hours they confessed their sins and worshiped the LORD their God. ~ Nehemiah 9:3

For it is by believing in your heart that you are made right with God, and it is by confessing with your mouth that you are saved. ~ Romans 10:10

But you, Timothy, are a man of God; so run from all these evil things. Pursue righteousness and a godly life, along with faith, love, perseverance, and gentleness. Fight the good fight for the true faith. Hold tightly to the eternal life to which God has called you, which you have confessed so well before many witnesses. ~ 1 Timothy 6:11-12

Fathers shall not be put to death for their sons, nor shall sons be put to death for their fathers; everyone shall be put to death for his own sin. ~ Deuteronomy 24:16

In place of your fathers will be your sons; You shall make them princes in all the earth. ~ Psalm 45:16

Hear, O sons, the instruction of a father, and give attention that you may gain understanding. ~ Proverbs 4:1

"It is you who are the sons of the prophets and of the covenant which God made with your fathers, saying to Abraham, ' and in your seed all the families of the earth shall be blessed.' ~ Acts 3:25

Day 20

I had another awesome devotion before the start of my day. My wife has been allowing me to come over and have dinner with her and the boys almost every evening. The boys love it and honestly, I do too. I miss them so much. I'm able to get caught up on how their day at school went and even help with some homework. They are awesome boys! I wish we didn't have so many distractions and outside influences so that I could be the dad they so greatly desire and need. I just want us to be a family once and for all!

My wife and I lost a baby last year. She began having pains in her stomach shortly after finding out we were pregnant. I didn't respond to her the way she needed me to when she was experiencing the pain so she ended up driving herself to the hospital and leaving the boys with me. I called several hours on the hour while they were running tests. Finally her mother came to get the boys so that I could be at the hospital with my wife. Once I arrived, we were told that we had a tubular pregnancy and the tube would have to be removed before it ruptured. We were devastated! I ministered to my wife. I told how much I loved her and how proud I was of her for being such a strong and beautiful woman. I told what an awesome mother I thought she was and knew she would be again. I ministered to my wife!

The doctor came in to explain the procedure and get us to sign our baby girl's life away. I just knew it was going to be a little girl. My wife kept talking, trying to tell jokes and pretending to be strong. I told her that it was okay and she had nothing to prove. I asked her to let me be strong for her. She finally let go and cried. I could feel the pain and disappointment that literally said, "I have failed as a woman and a mother! I have let my little girl down!" Nothing else mattered to me other than being there for my wife and our baby!

I prayed for her before they took her back for the surgery and was blessed to have the waiting room all to myself. Then, "It" began to hit me; we were losing our child! I had somehow, someway let my wife and our beautiful, innocent gift from God down! Was this more of the wrath from God that I had so arrogantly boasted that I could handle as I cowardly walked out of my last marriage? Was this God's way of saying that I had been such a terrible father and stepfather that I wouldn't have a chance to ruin this child's life? Was this a sign that things were so bad between my wife and me that no life could come forth or be sustained in our marriage? Had the stress that my wife was under caused this in some way? Had I screwed things up again???

I wished they were aborting me! I did not want to live. I could not live with the thought of "me" killing everything around me spiritually, emotionally and now physically. Lord if You are there, I need you now!

God literally caused a peace that I had never felt to come over me and I could hear Him as quietly and clearly as if He was speaking through an earpiece in my heart. He told me that He loved us. He told me that our child would never have to suffer a day in her life and would never feel pain. She would never taste death and was in His bosom right now. She was full of joy and loved us both very much! He said my mother and father would be with her and we would see her again one day soon. He then reminded me to love my wife as His Son loved the church.

It was at that very moment that the doctor walked in. She said the surgery had gone as expected and my wife would be fine. They had to totally remove one of her tubes, but the blessing was she still had the other one and we could still have children if we so desired! God is real and good!

When my wife opened her eyes I was right there. She tried to apologize to me for losing the baby; I told her she was still the most beautiful woman I had ever seen and that she was still all the woman I'd ever want or need. I told her what the doctor shared with me and that God had blessed us.

I felt like God was giving us another chance. I felt He was telling us to put all our faith in Him and trust

Him with everything in our marriage from this day forward! I felt He was telling us to forget the past and submit our lives to Him totally and completely from this day forward. I felt like this was another chance for me to be the husband and man He a called me to be. Man! I felt needed.

My Help for Day 20

But in my distress I cried out to the Lord; yes, I cried to my God for help. He heard me from his sanctuary; my cry reached his ears. ~ 2 Samuel 22:7

I cried out to the Lord, and he answered me from his holy mountain. ~ Psalm 3:4

In panic I cried out, "I am cut off from the Lord!" But you heard my cry for mercy and answered my call for help. ~ Psalm 31:22

I cried out, "I am slipping!" but your unfailing love, O Lord, supported me. ~ Psalm 94:18

If you return to the Almighty, you will be restored—so clean up your life. ~ Job 22:23

Then if my people who are called by my name will humble themselves and pray and seek my face and turn from their wicked ways, I will hear from heaven and will forgive their sins and restore their land. ~ 2 Chronicles 7:14

<u>Day 21</u>

There has been little change in my relationship. I am still feeling like more of a bother than a husband. However, there has been no change in my behavior either. I am "yet holding on," and refusing to let the behavior of others cause me to act unbecomingly.

I remember when my wife was getting out of the hospital after we lost the baby. My wife asked me to bring some things from the house when I came back to get her. I had been at the hospital all night by her bedside and was going home to get cleaned up, get her things and get back for her scheduled release. When I got home, I gathered everything that I needed to get, put it in a bag, and began taking my shower. That's when I fell apart!

Something about the water beating down on my head and my back hit me as if everything was about to come crashing down on top of me: losing our baby, my wife having to lose a part of her body, and all that we had been through in our marriage. I crashed! I needed help! I needed someone to minister to me for a minute! I needed someone to tell me it was going to be okay this time!

All of the previous "deaths" I had experienced, buried somewhere inside myself, but had not dealt with as my therapist had strongly encouraged me to deal with came flooding down on me with the water from the shower! They were still there! The death of my mother at an early age from cancer in over 80% of her body. She suffered greatly! The death of my Nanny who was like a mother to me – She was my mother's aunt and died of cancer like my mother! The death of my father who we found dead in his home from cancer, but who died alone! The death of my innocence due to multiple molestations! The death of my youth from having to deal with physical and mental abuse from my stepfather and having to just learn how to survive! The death of my integrity from: divorce, having a child out of wedlock, abusing and being abused by my current wife... *It all finally broke for me! I couldn't pretend anymore! The masks came off in the water! Now what? God why? Why now? Why me?*

I have to be honest; I did not pray. I couldn't. Nothing would come out! I was angry; I was hurt; I was crashing and burning, and I couldn't pray! I now know that I was mad at God again. I felt like He had allowed one of the worst things to happen in my life again – death of someone I loved and had not made everything okay. I still felt the pain and I didn't want to. I wanted everything to be okay right then and there; no process, no "time heals all wounds," no pain! I did the worst thing that I could do; I tried to get me together! The one who couldn't take care of his wife, his children, or his unborn child was now trying to get himself together? I had to...in my own mind!

So "Mr. Got-Myself-Together" made it back to hospital to "take care of" my wife who needed her husband so badly at that point in time only to realize that I had forgotten ALL of the things that she asked me to bring! I did not remember to get one of them! Yup, I got myself together alright!

I was so disappointed in myself and had the nerve to be defensive when my wife was disappointed in me too. She became a little short and somewhat impatient, but could I blame her?

I ended up leaving the room before I said something I shouldn't have. I wasn't angry at her. I was mad at myself for failing to pull it together; for not putting on a good front or a pretty mask; for not being the man that I thought I should be. Once again "Mr. Got-Myself-Together" was off to get himself together. However, still missing from the equation was the most important element-prayer!

I called her father, who was in town as a result of her surgery and whom she always ran to in order to make things better for her. Now I was about to do the same. I asked him if he would come to the hospital to pick her up. I told him that I felt like I was only making things worse and upsetting her at a time when she needed to be at peace. He didn't understand, but he agreed to come to get his daughter. I knew I had messed up again as soon as I hung the phone!

I went back to my wife's room to tell her "my" new game plan. As I tried to explain to her why I called her father, all I could think was "you are blowing it again!" Then I just wanted to tell her, "Baby I am falling apart! I need help! I don't know how to do this! I don't know how to make this okay!" Just then one of her friends walked into the room. I didn't say what I wanted to say, most import, what I needed to say to my wife. I felt like "here we go again!" Once again we couldn't just be... I left.

Looking back, I now realize that I could rise to the occasion, but never sustain the solution. Why? Because I was trying to do it by myself, and I couldn't do it! I was destined to fail every time I ventured out on my own to "fix" things myself. That trip was destined to be a journey to failure!

I realized that I had to honest with God right then and there. I had to tell Him that I was angry and why. He was big enough to handle it. I also had to admit who He was and who I was not-I was not in control! I could not fix anything; only He was able. I had to admit to that; I had to submit to that; and I had to accept that in every area of my life no matter what! I had to pray. Without prayer I was powerless. Without prayer I was lost. Without prayer I would stay angry and never be delivered.

I pray every morning, every night and several times throughout my day now. I quit trying to be deep and trying to pray those "spiritually verbose" prayers. In fact I feel like I have learned how to talk to my Father all over again. That's how I pray; we just talk. He talks and I listen, then I talk and He listens.

Now I am able to hear Him clearly before I try to be "Mr. Got-Myself-Together" and He directs my paths.

My Help for Day 21

Without consultation, plans are frustrated, But with many counselors they succeed. ~ Proverbs 15:22

You can make many plans, but the Lord's purpose will prevail. ~ Proverbs 19:21

So David said to God, "I have sinned greatly, because I have done this thing; but now, I pray, take away the iniquity of Your servant, for I have done very foolishly." ~ 1 Chronicles 21:8

I am the one who has sinned and done evil indeed; but these sheep, what have they done? Let Your hand, I pray, O LORD my God, be against me and my father's house, but not against Your people that they should be plagued. ~ 1 Chronicles 21:17

Therefore, let all the godly pray to you while there is still time, that they may not drown in the floodwaters of judgment. ~ Psalm 32:6

You don't let me sleep. I am too distressed even to pray! ~ Psalm 77:4

As soon as I pray, you answer me; you encourage me by giving me strength. ~ Psalm 138:3

Then you will call upon Me and come and pray to Me, and I will listen to you. ~ Jeremiah 29:12

Pray in the Spirit at all times and on every occasion. Stay alert and be persistent in your prayers for all believers everywhere. ~ Ephesians 6:18

We also pray that you will be strengthened with all his glorious power so you will have all the endurance and patience you need. May you be filled with joy, ~ Colossians 1:11

In every place of worship, I want men to pray with holy hands lifted up to God, free from anger and controversy. ~ 1 Timothy 2:8

Are any of you suffering hardships? You should pray. Are any of you happy? You should sing praises. ~ James 5:13

The end of all things is near. Therefore be clear minded and self-controlled so that you can pray. ~ 1 Peter 4:7

But you, dear friends, must build each other up in your most holy faith, pray in the power of the Holy Spirit, and await the mercy of our Lord Jesus Christ, who will bring you eternal life. In this way, you will keep yourselves safe in God's love. ~ Jude 1:20-21

Day 22

Well I finally met the "new friend." I have to admit I didn't know what to expect, but I have been praying every time his name came up which was often. I was fine at first, but something didn't seem right in my spirit. I don't want to bear false witness against anyone anymore so I can't say that I knew his true intentions, but the old me would have lost it! I'm not a jealous person, but when all I have been hearing is "he said this" and "he said that" every time my wife and I have had a conversation over the past week or more, my mind began to think this is some mess! I found myself getting angry because I had been asked to step down from my church and give up all involvement with ministry to work on our marriage, but my wife seemed to be working more on this "friendship" than our marriage! Couple those feelings with the fact my wife was acting like a giddy schoolgirl around this person and it was very noticeable!

These are the types of conditions that I would allow blind rage to have its way in me and with me, but not anymore! I never woke up and said "It's Tuesday and I haven't beat my wife today." What I did was not control myself when a bunch of mess was thrown in our lives, our marriage or my face and I lost control of me!

It was cowardly, childish behavior and I am ashamed of myself! I understand there was never an excuse or reason that justified me yelling at, cussing out or any type of aggressive, ungodly, violent behavior with my wife regardless of what she did or said!

The blessing to us in this situation was the fact I could see it happening literally in slow motion! I could see the pitfalls and the traps. I could see the right path and the wrong one and I had time to make the right choice! So I did! I did not use it as an opportunity to blame them for my inappropriate behavior. I wasn't going to make calls to my "friends" saying "My wife and her friend made me act like a fool today! I had to get them straight!" I was able to give God all the glory for showing me my mistakes from the past and my choices for my present. TO HIM BE ALL THE GLORY!!!

In addition to the way my wife's behavior appeared to me, she was clearly much more excited about introducing him to "her" boys than her family - husband included. In fact, there were a couple of other people that she failed to introduce me to even though I was standing right there.

Once again, God showed me to myself. That behavior use to be one of her biggest complaints about me; I'd greet and speak to someone and fail to introduce her properly. I explained to her that if I didn't, it was simply because I didn't remember their names. After several complaints, I started introducing her whether I remembered their names or not because I didn't want to slight the person that I loved. Now I had a first hand view of how it really felt and I didn't like it at all!

It was really hard to lose my temper over my perception that something wasn't right when God was showing me my own shortcomings. I found myself praying earnestly for forgiveness, for this gentleman & his family (he is married with children) and for my wife. I didn't think I was better than anyone, but I knew I had to do what I was supposed to do as a husband regardless of whatever else was going on.

Once again, I was being spoken to in a very short and impatient manner, and was even told to "just leave" at one point. As I started walking away, I clearly heard the Lord tell me to stand still and be whom I was called to be. I went back and apologized for anything that I said or did to upset my wife. I'm not sure how happy she was, but the boys were excited that I came back and spent the rest of the day with them as a "family".

I was glad to finally be doing what God had told me to do without regard to anything or anyone else. As long as I focused on Him, I was okay. If I allowed myself to pay attention to what was being said to me or what was going on around me, I felt the pain. It was that simple.

I was reminded of something God spoke to me the last time I was crying about our marriage, "I can take care of her and the marriage, what I really want now is you." He has me, my obedience, my attention, my direction and my focus…now.

Man! Who did I meet today, my wife's new friend or my True Best Friend? GOD!

My Help for Day 22

You will keep in perfect peace all who trust in you, all whose thoughts are fixed on you! ~ Isaiah 26:3

Look at those who are honest and good, for a wonderful future awaits those who love peace. ~ Psalm 37:37

Dear brothers and sisters, I close my letter with these last words: Be joyful. Grow to maturity. Encourage each other. Live in harmony and peace. Then the God of love and peace will be with you. ~ 2 Corinthians 13:11

"I will confirm my covenant with you and your descendants after you, from generation to generation. This is the everlasting covenant: I will always be your God and the God of your descendants after you. ~ Genesis 17:7

If you listen to what I tell you and follow my ways and do whatever I consider to be right, and if you obey my decrees and commands, as my servant David did, then I will always be with you. ~ 1 Kings 11:38a

I know the Lord is always with me. I will not be shaken, for he is right beside me. ~ Psalm 16:8

May you always be filled with the fruit of your salvation—the righteous character produced in your life by Jesus Christ —for this will bring much glory and praise to God. ~ Philippians 1:11

Teaching them to observe everything that I have commanded you, and behold, I am with you all the days (perpetually, uniformly, and on every occasion), to the [very] close and consummation of the age. Amen (so let it be). ~ Matthew 28:20

The man of many friends [a friend of all the world] will prove himself a bad friend, but there is a friend who sticks closer than a brother. ~ Proverbs 18:24

Day 23

My therapist asked me when I realized the spirit of rage no longer had control over me. Good question! I hadn't actually given it much thought, but all of a sudden I was excited at the realization...I was no longer controlled by my anger! I was no longer out of control! To God be the glory! I thank God for the revelation, but now I have to do the one thing that was most difficult and painful for me: take an in-depth look at what was going on inside of me...

I realized that I have felt rejected and discarded because of the poor choices that I've made. I felt like people that I either cared about or trusted to help me judged me, turned their backs, and ultimately gave up on me. I let the things I heard from my wife, her family and friends like, "Once an abuser, always an abuser" get into my spirit and literally make me believe those very words myself! I had been praying for things that I honestly had doubts about myself; that I could truly repent, be forgiven and finally be delivered! *I wanted that more than anything!*

I wanted to stop hurting everyone I cared about physically, mentally and spiritually, and I wanted to stop hurting myself! I did! I felt instant pain and remorse. *That was not good enough!* "I'm sorry" didn't have enough letters in it or power to make up for what I had done to her! In fact it was true, I was sorry; *A sorry excuse for a man!*

The same God I had been so angry with for allowing so much "death" in my life had allowed yet another one to affect me; *the death of my rage!* He was the same God I needed to now trust for my deliverance. He had answered my prayers. I was tired of fighting Him. I began to stop whining and started listening to the One who made me. This was my death and resurrection; I had finally allowed my flesh to be killed and Him to resurrect me to be who He wanted me to be!

He took me back to the *truth* and to the truth about me. The truth is I was not born to be an abuser *and* I was not going to die as one either!

Without pointing fingers or trying to lay blame on anyone else, I had to go back to some truths: I never put my hands on my first wife. (The one that I put away without cause!); the first blows passed in this relationship were not initiated by me. She slapped me twice in front of several of my church members before we got married because I asked her to leave due to her inappropriate language and behavior in front of some of the young people.

I didn't hit her back when: she spit in my face (This literally stripped me of my humanity. I felt like a dog!); she hit me in head with a phone and damaged my eardrum; she destroyed expensive property and meaningful pictures of my mother and family; I found out that she moved us in the same neighborhood as her ex-lover whom she was dating openly while we were married; she threw my cancer up in my face as a weapon in front of her family; she slapped and hit me repeatedly while I was driving to a ministry event and then threatened to call the police on me and say that I hit her! (For the first time I cancelled my role in the event rather than put on a mask and act like everything was okay!); she hit me with my car; or when she beat me to a bloody mess and stabbed me repeatedly with car keys...

When I, the abuser, became the abused...something broke in me and for me! *I now knew how it felt! And I didn't like what I was feeling!* I shut down. I didn't want her to touch me even to comfort me. I definitely didn't want to be kissed, held or made love to by her! I didn't want to hear her say she was sorry. I was hurt physically, but I was most hurt mentally and spiritually! A part of me died where she was concerned. A part of me was beaten out of me by her. I lost something that I was not sure I could ever regain! I was numb. I didn't know who I was. I had try to regain my identity! I had to start loving myself all over again!

I realized once and for all I didn't know my real value and understood that I didn't value her highly at all when I did the same to her. I came face-to-face with the very thing that I had become – an abuser, and I didn't like it! *It had to stop that day!*

The truth of the whole rage and anger matter is the fact that there is self-control in me…I just need to use it in every situation. No matter what! God was now in control. He was truly my Guide. I was finally willing to exhibit the fruit of the Spirit – self-control.

It finally started to make sense; the truth was I was doing things that I didn't have to do and had choices/power/control to not do them. God I was not born to be an abuser *and* I was not going to die as one either!

The real truth is, I was not born to be molested, be abused, not have affection, be told I'd never be anything, be married multiple times, be divorced ever, be in several meaningless sexual relationships, have a child out of wedlock, not have real friendships, have filed bankruptcy, have been diagnosed with cancer and not have a real, personal relationship with Christ!

The same God that made my accusers and judges made me with purpose, promise, provision and destiny too! I need to accept that, address my unaddressed issues, get up and walk into what has been prepared AND promised to me! I could keep listening to them point out every mistake I've made in the short time that they've know me and use their negative reports to define who I was; OR, I could finally start listening to, believing in and walking in what God was saying about my entire life. *It is time!*

The only thing that was stopping me was me! I have to stop sabotaging my future with behavior from my past. I have to stop using my past as excuses for my present behavior.

This was a turning point for me. This is when it changed and stayed changed. I didn't need help to restore my marriage. I need help to restore my life! I finally realized a restored life would lead to restored relationships of all kinds; restoration in a right relationship with God first and foremost! I had to ask myself after receiving that kind of restoration, did I even want a restored relationship with someone (my wife) who has yet to even begin this journey for herself. This is a journey she, and anyone who has ever been an abuser, *will* have to take! However, my prayer for her is she won't be thrown away, discarded and given up on like she is willing to do with me.

THERE IS VALUE IN ME! I HAVE WORTH! I AM YIELDED TO GOD'S PERFECT WILL! GOD HAS USE FOR ME IN HIS KINGDOM!

She may be throwing me away, but God is rummaging through the trash looking for me! I can hear Him say, "Someone threw him away? I was looking for one just like him!" I can feel Him taking me home, cleaning me up, fixing what is broken and making me better! I can feel Him putting me back on track and saying, "Run on and sin no more!" *THANK YOU, FATHER! THANK YOU! THANK YOU!*

I made a choice and I am not changing my mind...*I AM NOT GOING TO LET THE OLD ME KILL THE BORN AGAIN ME!*

<u>My Help for Day 23</u>

And you will know the truth, and the truth will make you free. ~ John 8:32

So if the Son sets you free, you are truly free. ~ John 8:36

If it seems we are crazy, it is to bring glory to God. And if we are in our right minds, it is for your benefit. Either way, Christ's love controls us. Since we believe that Christ died for all, we also believe that we have all died to our old life. He died for everyone so that those who receive his new life will no longer live for themselves. Instead, they will live for Christ, who died and was raised for them. ~ 2 Corinthians 5:13-15

An evil man is held captive by his own sins; they are ropes that catch and hold him. He will die for lack of self-control; he will be lost because of his great foolishness. ~ Proverbs 5:22-23

But the Holy Spirit produces this kind of fruit in our lives: love, joy, peace, patience, kindness, goodness, faithfulness, gentleness, and self-control. There is no law against these things! Those who belong to Christ Jesus have nailed the passions and desires of their sinful nature to his cross and crucified them there. ~ Galatians 5:22-24

Well then, should we keep on sinning so that God can show us more and more of his wonderful grace? Of course not! Since we have died to sin, how can we continue to live in it? ~ Romans 6:1-2

For we died and were buried with Christ by baptism. And just as Christ was raised from the dead by the glorious power of the Father, now we also may live new lives. ~ Romans 6:4

We know that our old sinful selves were crucified with Christ so that sin might lose its power in our lives. We are no longer slaves to sin. 7 For when we died with

Christ we were set free from the power of sin. ~ Romans 6:6-7

When he died, he died once to break the power of sin. But now that he lives, he lives for the glory of God. So you also should consider yourselves to be dead to the power of sin and alive to God through Christ Jesus. ~ Romans 6:10-11

Do not let sin control the way you live; do not give in to sinful desires. Do not let any part of your body become an instrument of evil to serve sin. Instead, give yourselves completely to God, for you were dead, but now you have new life. So use your whole body as an instrument to do what is right for the glory of God. Sin is no longer your master, for you no longer live under the requirements of the law. Instead, you live under the freedom of God's grace. ~ Romans 6:12-14

Well then, since God's grace has set us free from the law, does that mean we can go on sinning? Of course not! ~ Romans 6:15

Day 24

God, how did I get so far off of Your perfect (mature) plan for my life? You never left me; how and why did I leave You? You made me better than I've carried myself. Why did I think it was okay living beneath Your standards *over and over and over and over and over again?*

One of the things that of all the things that happened to me in the past accomplished was to make me lose focus. (this sentence needs rewriting for clarity) They distracted me and caused me to miss/delay becoming who I was supposed to be, who I had to help me and what I needed most...GOD THE FATHER, JESUS HIS SON and THE COMFORTER, HIS HOLY SPIRIT!!!

I now understand that I was so distracted at an early age, by "stuff" and that's all it was...stuff! It was bad stuff, but it was just stuff. I can't keep giving that stuff more power than it deserves. It was bad stuff, but it didn't make me a bad person. It was stuff that didn't define who I was and certainly not who I was going to be!

I had to realize the stuff had caused me to misunderstand what a father's love looked and felt like. As a result, I couldn't truly understand the Father's love if I never felt a father's love in my life. I was distracted by stuff in my natural life, *so I couldn't receive the Father's love in my spiritual life!*

I heard preacher after preacher saying, "The Father loves you! The Father loves you!" I found myself saying okay and even repeating it to others, but I still didn't know what it really meant or even looked like myself! *I had never seen it!* I was going through the motions, but ending up at the same place...LOST and HURTING!!!

I finally started reading God's Word; not to get a word to give to someone else, but to understand Him for myself. After Ministers training, Bible College and

Seminary, working on staff at churches, being ordained as an apostle over several churches and finally pastoring my own church, I was finally learning what the Father's love meant for my life. I love it! I love the way it feels! THANK YOU GOD FOR LOVING ME IN SPITE OF ME!!!

Now I not only understand the Father's love, but I depend on it. His love has allowed me to appreciate and accept my natural father's love. Even more profound, His love has allowed me to accept my abusive stepfather's love as well. Both did the best they could with what they had. They had issues just like I did. They didn't have good examples or role models on what being fathers, priests, protectors and providers for their homes either. They were hurting just like me! Now I can forgive them because of the Father's love. While my wife is falling out of love with me, the Father is reminding me there is *NOTHING* I can do to make Him stop.

Man! It is time for me to let go of and put away my stuff once and for all.

My Help for Day 24

I look up to the mountains—does my help come from there? My help comes from the LORD, who made heaven and earth! He will not let you stumble; the one who watches over you will not slumber. ~ Psalm 121:1-3

I call heaven and earth to witness this day against you that I have set before you life and death, the blessings and the curses; therefore choose life, that you and your descendants may live and may love the Lord your God, obey His voice, and cling to Him. For He is your life and the length of your days, that you may dwell in the land which the Lord swore to give to your fathers, to Abraham, Isaac, and Jacob. ~ Deuteronomy 30:19-21

So be strong and courageous! Do not be afraid and do not panic before them. For the LORD your God will personally go ahead of you. He will neither fail you nor abandon you. ~ Deuteronomy 31:6

Do not be afraid or discouraged, for the LORD will personally go ahead of you. He will be with you; he will neither fail you nor abandon you. ~ Deuteronomy 31:8

May the LORD our God be with us as he was with our fathers; may he never leave us nor forsake us. ~ 1 Kings 8:57

And I will give them one heart and one purpose: to worship me forever, for their own good and for the good of all their descendants. And I will make an everlasting covenant with them: I will never stop doing good for them. I will put a desire in their hearts to worship me, and they will never leave me. I will find joy doing good for them and will faithfully and wholeheartedly replant them in this land. ~ Jeremiah 32:39-41

And I will ask the Father, and he will give you another Advocate, who will never leave you. ~ John 14:16

Dear friends, never take revenge. Leave that to the righteous anger of God. For the Scriptures say, "I will take revenge; I will pay them back," says the Lord. ~ Romans 12:19

Let your character or moral disposition be free from love of money [including greed, avarice, lust, and craving for earthly possessions] and be satisfied with your present [circumstances and with what you have]; for He [God] Himself has said, I will not in any way fail you nor give you up nor leave you without support. [I will] not, [I will] not, [I will] not in any degree leave you helpless nor forsake nor let [you] down (relax My hold on you)! [Assuredly not!] ~ Hebrews 13:5

When I was a child, I spoke and thought and reasoned as a child. But when I grew up, I put away childish things. ~ 1 Corinthians 13:11

Day 25

Thanks be to God!!! My wife has been allowing me to come over before she goes to work so that I can be there when the boys wake up. I've been helping them get dressed, preparing their breakfast and lunches and taking them to school. We have had a great time!!! We've made up songs, learned how to yoyo, practiced spelling words (received 100's I might add!), and of course gone over homework. We even have great devotion when they get home from school before they start watching television AND THEY LOOK FORWARD TO IT! I feel like God is blessing me with them and them with a new me. TO GOD BE THE GLORY! I AM IN HEAVEN!

After I drop the boys off, I have been going back to my wife's place to take care of whatever needs to be done: the laundry – washed and folded; dishes – washed and put away; kitchen – cleaned! Whatever needs to be done!!! I want my wife, who has been working 12 hour days 7 days a week, and my boys to be able to come home to a clean house and relax! I want there to be peace waiting for them when they walk in the door.

I'm no longer concerned or motivated by what she is or is not doing. I have responsibility and control over my own behavior and I choose to be the best husband and father I can be. I can't keep worrying about what other people are saying about whether or not we should still be together or how bad I've messed up in the past. I CAN'T CHANGE IT! IT IS WHAT IT IS! All I have control over is right now and I pray without ceasing for God to allow me to make the most of it. I feel released to be who God made me to be. I feel forgiven. I feel redeemed. Not by people, but by the One Who made them. I feel free to be *His* best husband, father and man. I can feel *His* encouragement to listen to *His* instructions and directions not be paralyzed by my past mistakes and poor choices.

I can see Him and His approval in the smiles on the faces of the boys. I can hear His joy in their laughter from deep down in their bellies. I know He is pleased when I hear them say, "Thank you, Daddy!" for the little things I was doing for them and with them. I could feel His love through them and I refuse to miss it by looking back or too far ahead at what MIGHT happen.

My wife has even thanked me for what I've been doing. That's not necessary because it's what I should have been doing all along, but I appreciate the fact that she noticed. God has blessed me to strengthen my relationship with my own boys as well. We have had conference calls with each other where we laughed and I could literally feel their joy, love and happiness coming through the phones; just because we were on the phone together. I have been able to speak life into and tell them how proud I was of who they were and were becoming in spite of me. Not to be out done, they have poured life in me for the change that both of them have been able to see! We are loving each other and LOVING EVERY MINUTE OF IT!

I feel like their priest, protector and provider and it feels GOOOOOOOOD!!!

My Help for Day 25

Make thankfulness your sacrifice to God, and keep the vows you made to the Most High. ~ Psalm 50:14

So be careful how you live. Don't live like fools, but like those who are wise. Make the most of every opportunity in these evil days. Don't act thoughtlessly, but understand what the Lord wants you to do. ~ Ephesians 5:15-17

Pray that I may proclaim it clearly, as I should. Be wise in the way you act toward outsiders; make the most of every opportunity. Let your conversation be always full of grace, seasoned with salt, so that you may know how to answer everyone. ~ Colossians 4:4-6

And you must commit yourselves wholeheartedly to these commands that I am giving you today. Repeat them again and again to your children. Talk about them when you are at home and when you are on the road, when you are going to bed and when you are getting up. ~ Deuteronomy 6:6-7

"But watch out! Be careful never to forget what you yourself have seen. Do not let these memories escape from your mind as long as you live! And be sure to pass them on to your children and grandchildren. ~ Deuteronomy 4:9

If your children will keep My covenant and My testimony that I shall teach them, their children also shall sit upon your throne forever. Psalm 132:12

For the LORD sees clearly what a man does, examining every path he takes. An evil man is held captive by his own sins; they are ropes that catch and hold him. He will die for lack of self-control; he will be lost because of his great foolishness. ~ Proverbs 5:21-23

Turn away from evil and do good. Search for peace, and work to maintain it. ~ Psalm 34:14

Stop being angry! Turn from your rage! Do not lose your temper—it only leads to harm. ~ Psalm 37:8

The LORD directs the steps of the godly. He delights in every detail of their lives. Though they stumble, they will never fall, for the LORD holds them by the hand. ~ Psalm 37:23-24

Once I was young, and now I am old. Yet I have never seen the godly abandoned or their children begging for bread. ~ Psalm 37:25

Look at those who are honest and good, for a wonderful future awaits those who love peace. ~ Psalm 37:37

So all of us who have had that veil removed can see and reflect the glory of the Lord. And the Lord—who is the Spirit—makes us more and more like him as we are changed into his glorious image. ~ 2 Corinthians 3:18

And the nations shall see your righteousness and vindication [your rightness and justice--not your own, but His ascribed to you], and all kings shall behold your salvation and glory; and you shall be called by a new name which the mouth of the Lord shall name. ~ Isaiah 62:2

For the Lord God is our sun and our shield. He gives us grace and glory. The Lord will withhold no good thing from those who do what is right. ~ Psalm 84:11

Day 26

Well what do you know??? My wife gave me my own key to her place. To God be the glory!!! She's even talking about where she wants us to live when "we get through all of this." She's obviously been thinking about things because she talked about both of our leases ending about the same time and that we should be saving our money for a down payment on our house! We've also talked about getting her a new car. I'm just happy she is saying "we" and is thinking about "us!"

Needless to say I thank God for His grace and mercy. He has truly answered my prayers! I am going to continue to do my part and what I have been doing: seeking His will and direction at the start of every day through His Word, prayer, praise, worship and devotion, loving her unconditionally like Christ loved the church REGARDLESS of what she does or how she responds, being the best priest, protector and provider for all of our boys, praying for my wife and children in the Spirit, showing them "Love" is an action word, and knowing God is taking care of all of my needs!

This hasn't been easy. I have had to go to the Lord in prayer plenty of times. I've had to tell My Daddy all about my problems! I have not been able to share most of this experience with anyone for several reasons: I don't listen to anyone who tells me to leave or divorce my wife; I don't want to get my family and friends worried or upset, then my wife and I work things out and they are still upset – we've both made that mistake in the past! God is the only one with the answers so why go anywhere else? That has never worked for me!

This is a faith walk. It's my faith walk. I have done it wrong every single time before now. I have never done it right. I have given up. I have taken the easy way out. I found people who empowered me to do it my way; even if my way was the wrong way. I had to finally do something different to end up in a different place. I had enough of my own experiences and wisdom to know that the old way did not work. Wisdom unapplied is foolishness! This time it is God's way and His way alone.

This time if I mess up, I run to Him to get cleaned up! If I fail, I run to Him to get restored. If I'm confused, I run to Him for clarity and if I'm discouraged, I run to Him to get encouraged. I do not only trust Him now, He is my only choice! I'm not saying it's easy, but it does get easier, and it is better than anything I ever tried before. Plain and simple, there is no more plan b; in fact, there is no more plan "me!"

Thank you Father. Today was a good day.

My Help for Day 26

And this same God who takes care of me will supply all your needs from his glorious riches, which have been given to us in Christ Jesus. Now all glory to God our Father forever and ever! Amen. ~ Philippians 4:19-20

God gave Solomon very great wisdom and understanding, and knowledge as vast as the sands of the seashore. ~ 1 Kings 4:29

Give me the wisdom and knowledge to lead them properly, for who could possibly govern this great people of yours?" God said to Solomon, "Because your greatest desire is to help your people, and you did not ask for wealth, riches, fame, or even the death of your enemies or a long life, but rather you asked for wisdom and knowledge to properly govern my people—I will certainly give you the wisdom and knowledge you requested. But I will also give you wealth, riches, and fame such as no other king has had before you or will ever have in the future!" ~ 2 Chronicles 1:10-12

Teach us to realize the brevity of life, so that we may grow in wisdom. ~ Psalm 90:12

Then you will understand what it means to fear the LORD, and you will gain knowledge of God. For the LORD grants wisdom! From his mouth come knowledge and understanding. He grants a treasure of common sense to the honest. He is a shield to those who walk with integrity. Proverbs 2:5-7

He guards the paths of the just and protects those who are faithful to him. Then you will understand what is right, just, and fair, and you will find the right way to go. For wisdom will enter your heart, and knowledge will fill you with joy. Wise choices will watch over you. Understanding will keep you safe. ~ Proverbs 2:8-11

Joyful is the person who finds wisdom, the one who gains understanding. For wisdom is more profitable than silver, and her wages are better than gold. ~ Proverbs 3:13-14

Dear children, let's not merely say that we love each other; let us show the truth by our actions. Our actions will show that we belong to the truth, so we will be confident when we stand before God. ~ 1 John 3:18-19

"The LORD is my rock, my fortress, and my savior; my God is my rock, in whom I find protection. He is my shield, the power that saves me, and my place of safety. He is my refuge, my savior, the one who saves me from violence. ~ 2 Samuel 22:2-3

And [I charge] the husband [also] that he should not put away or divorce his wife. ~ 1 Corinthians 7:11b

Let all the world look to Me for salvation! For I am God; there is no other. I have sworn by My own Name; I have spoken the truth, and I will never go back on My word: Every knee will bend to Me, and every tongue will confess allegiance to Me." The people will declare, "The LORD is the source of all My righteousness and strength." ~ Isaiah 45:22-24

I will give thanks to You, O Lord my God, with all my heart, and will glorify Your name forever. Psalm 86:12

Day 27

Another day, additional revelations... God showed me I turned an "I said" into a "God said;" at least I tried to anyway. When I first saw my wife, I said, "That could be my wife." I never heard God say, "That *is* your wife." I then proceeded to go about making her my wife. I tried to justify it by the fact that I never lusted after my wife or approached her in an inappropriate way, but it was still an "I said," not a "God said." Therefore I was operating outside of His will for my life.

What I have since come to understand is simply this: *IF I AM NOT IN GOD'S WILL, I AM ON MY OWN!* And *THAT'S A DANGEROUS PLACE TO BE!* Even worse is than that: *MY WILL + MY WAY - GOD = DISASTER!!!*

A disaster is exactly what I made of my wife's life, the lives of our children, the lives of our family, the lives of our closest friends, the lives of my members and my own life as well all because I tried to turn an "I said" into a "God said"! Why? Why did I try to do that? Why did I mess up the lives of sooo many people trying to disguise what I wanted under what God promised? I had been in a "serious" relationship since my sophomore year of high school with very few breaks right up to this marriage that I am in now...That's over 27 years!

I DID NOT WANT TO BE ALONE! I was molested when I was alone! I was abused when I was alone! I was lonely when I was alone! I felt abandoned when I was alone! I felt helpless when I was alone! I felt vulnerable, scared, useless and without promise when I was alone! I didn't feel like a man when I was alone! I didn't want to die alone! My mother died estranged from my stepfather! My father died alone!

I was hurting, hiding and trying to cover up my pain in the life of a relationship. I could just try to be what she wanted me to be and not have to be who I was! I didn't have to face my miserable life; I could just start a new one with her. I could forget the past and never address it again… WRONG! WRONG!! WRONG!!!

I am not blaming my parents because I know they loved me the best they could in the state they were in. However, the truth of the matter is, my mother was married and divorced three times and my father was married and divorced four times. *I had issues that needed to be addressed before I ever tried to date, get engaged, married or even have children!* I tried to make a bunch of what "I said" and wanted into what "God said" and wanted for me. I am finally seeing the price that was paid and the pain caused by me not dealing with me.

Being totally honest…I didn't want to hear what "God said" during most of all of this either. Plenty of people had a word for me, advice for me, prophecy about how blessed I'd be and anointed I was, and drive by scripture quotes for me:

"This too shall pass.""They that wait upon the Lord shall renew their strength…"

"God knows what you need before you even need it."

"He may not come when you want Him, but He's always on time." Etc., etc., etc., etc!!!

I DIDN'T WANT TO HEAR IT! I JUST WANTED TO MAKE MY PAST, MY PAIN, AND MY ISSUES GO AWAY!

I just wanted to be happy, and have what I didn't have growing up...a happy family. Now I realize I went about it all wrong each and every time. I did it my way and God let me have it my way. One thing I am certain of...my way doesn't work.

God, never again will I try to present what I want as what You said. If You don't say it, I don't want it. That's how my past, my pain and issues will change, and even if they don't, the way I perceive them will. In the name of Jesus. Amen.

My Help for Day 27

The LORD gave this message to Jonah son of Amittai: "Get up and go to the great city of Nineveh. Announce my judgment against it because I have seen how wicked its people are." But Jonah got up and went in the opposite direction to get away from the LORD. He went down to the port of Joppa, where he found a ship leaving for Tarshish. He bought a ticket and went on board, hoping to escape from the LORD by sailing to Tarshish. But the LORD hurled a powerful wind over the sea, causing a violent storm that threatened to break the ship apart. Fearing for their lives, the desperate sailors shouted to their gods for help and threw the cargo overboard to lighten the ship. But all this time Jonah was sound asleep down in the hold. ~ Jonah 1:1-5

Then Jonah prayed to the LORD his God from inside the fish. He said, "I cried out to the LORD in my great trouble, and he answered me. I called to you from the land of the dead, and LORD, you heard me! ~ Jonah 2:1-2

Is this the way you repay the LORD, you foolish and senseless people? Isn't he your Father who created you? Has he not made you and established you? Remember the days of long ago; think about the generations past. Ask your father, and he will inform you. Inquire of your elders, and they will tell you. ~ Deuteronomy 32:6-7

Listen to me, descendants of Jacob, all you who remain in Israel. I have cared for you since you were born. Yes, I carried you before you were born. I will be your God throughout your lifetime — until your hair is white with age. I made you, and I will care for you. I will carry you along and save you. ~ Isaiah 46:3-4

Listen to me, you stubborn people who are so far from doing right. For I am ready to set things right, not in the distant future, but right now! ~ Isaiah 46:12-13a

This is what the LORD says — your Redeemer, the Holy One of Israel: "I am the LORD your God, who teaches you what is good for you and leads you along the paths you should follow. Oh, that you had listened to my commands! Then you would have had peace flowing like a gentle river and righteousness rolling over you like waves in the sea. Your descendants would have been like the sands along the seashore—too many to count! There would have been no need for your destruction, or for cutting off your family name." ~ Isaiah 48:17-19

None of their past sins will be brought up again, for they have done what is just and right, and they will surely live. ~ Ezekiel 33:16

They will accept responsibility for their past shame and unfaithfulness after they come home to live in peace in their own land, with no one to bother them. ~ Ezekiel 39:26

"Father, if You are willing, please take this cup of suffering away from me. Yet I want Your will to be done, not mine." Then an angel from heaven appeared and strengthened him. ~ Luke 22:42-43

Day 28

I brought a futon mattress over to my wife so that I could sleep on the floor and be with my family as much as I possibly can. I have given my wife massages to help ease her tension from her 12 hour days and I have made love to her every night this week exactly the way she desired.

I am determined to be the best husband and lover of her soul I can be while I have a chance. Her words to me were, "I feel like you are falling in love with making love to your wife again." I am. Now I could make love to her because I love myself. I'm no longer trying to make up for past problems, (molestation, proving I was a man, loneliness, broken promises or relationships, etc.) or mistakes (abuse, lies, failure to be a priest, protector and provider). I could love my wife because I loved my wife.

If I want this to end differently from my other relationships, I have to do things differently. Normally I would have become frustrated and discouraged and given up. I would have tried to justify my giving up with her actions. NOT THIS TIME!

We have a confession in our new church: "My flesh is disciplined. Therefore where I have need, I will change!" I understand that I have to be disciplined within this marriage to have a chance for change in this marriage. I have to be disciplined in my behavior to experience change in my behavior. I don't want to end up like I have in the past. I NEED TO CHANGE!

God has not allowed me to see myself, my past and my mistakes for me to stay the same. He has brought about the change; now I need to walk like, think like, talk like and live like I am changed; not faking it, but living it.

I love the way she is responding to me physically, mentally and spiritually. For the first time in a long time, I feel like a

Day 29

I have been so blessed by my early morning devotion, prayer, praise and worship. I have even grown to the place where I simply sit still and listen; not sleep, or tell God what I want Him to do for me in this situation, but I simply listen.

One thing I clearly heard was I didn't get here overnight or because of one specific incident and I will not get out of it overnight either. I usually look for the easiest way out with the least amount of pain possible. However, I heard clearly that while this might hurt for a while, I was going to make it out. Most importantly, I was never going to be the same. The situation may be the same, but the way I looked at it, thought about it, felt about it, reacted to it was all going to be different from this day forward.

All of my past excuses and ways of escape: blaming others, blaming my past, lies, running to other relationships before dealing with or ending the difficult one, pretending everything was okay, being a hypocrite, etc… These were not going to work any longer, thus I needed to get rid of them.

I heard loud and clear, "It is time to come clean." Coming clean for me didn't just mean to reveal the things I had not revealed, it also meant I had to go through a cleaning process. I literally had to "become clean." Again, I had been dirty and living foul for so long, I had to go through a spiritual, mental and physical cleansing process to stay free from the old me.

God had not shown me all that He had shown me over the past 30 days for me to "act" like I was clean. It was time for me to be cleansed from all unrighteousness; whether I did it or if it was done to me. What? The things done to me defined who I was! How was I now going to be cleaned from those things and just let them go? Who was I going to be if I let go of the things which defined me?

I would no longer have any excuses for my anger, sooo I would have no need to be angry...I would no longer have an excuse to lash out at my wife, so I would no longer lash out at my wife! God, I am starting to get this!!! It actually makes sense. If I don't have the excuses as a crutch, then I won't have any justification at all for the behavior. Once I put the excuse to rest, then I can bury the behavior once and for all.

While I understand what I'm hearing and am excited about the possibilities of being free once and for all, I am actually scared to death! I have not been a good man, father, husband, pastor, brother or son, but the truth is, I've only been what I knew how to be. How do I let go of everything I know to become and do that which I don't know? What if I fail? Who's going to walk me through this? How long will it take? GOD?

I know that I can't stay the same. In fact, I have enjoyed the changes that have already taken place in me. Can't that just be enough? I'm realizing that I have to go all the way so that I'll never even be tempted to go back to the old me. I also realize that this cleaning needs to take place whether my wife and I are restored or not. I can't live the rest of my life making excuses for my inappropriate behavior nor can I expect people to understand because of my past. *WHAT HAPPENED TO ME WAS NOT MY FAULT, BUT THEY ARE MY CIRCUMSTANCES, SO I HAVE TO DEAL WITH THEM!*

My therapist actually confirmed what I heard God say, "The only way I can deal with my circumstances is to stop looking for acceptance and approval from others and just deal." I have been guilty of that for far too long. That has been the source of my problems for several years; not feeling accepted or approved. Thus I tried to find it in the wrong relationships with the wrong people in the wrong way at the wrong time! IT DOESN'T WORK! Then I feel better and try to hit a "light switch" and turn on being good, healthy and whole again and I'm not. IT DOESN'T WORK!

I heard loud and clear, "It is time to come clean." It's time to do it for myself because it's the right thing to do; not because it will save my marriage, or make anyone else like/love me. It's time to come clean.

Father, have Your way in the name of Jesus. Amen!

My Help for Day 29

When the man with the discharge is healed, he must count off seven days for the period of purification. Then he must wash his clothes and bathe himself in fresh water, and he will be ceremonially clean. ~ Leviticus 15:13

On that day offerings of purification will be made for you, and you will be purified in the LORD's presence from all your sins. ~ Leviticus 16:30

The righteous keep moving forward, and those with clean hands become stronger and stronger. ~ Job 17:9

If you return to the Almighty, you will be restored — so clean up your life. ~ Job 22:23

Wash me clean from my guilt. Purify me from my sin. ~ Psalm 51:2

Purify me from my sins, and I will be clean; wash me, and I will be whiter than snow. ~ Psalm 51:7

Create in me a clean heart, O God. Renew a loyal spirit within me. Psalm 51:10

Wash yourselves and be clean! Get your sins out of my sight. Give up your evil ways. ~ Isaiah 1:16

So the angel said to the others standing there, "Take off his filthy clothes." And turning to Jeshua he said, "See, I have taken away your sins, and now I am giving you these fine new clothes." Then I said, "They should also place a clean turban on his head." So they put a clean priestly turban on his head and dressed him in new clothes while the angel of the LORD stood by. Then the angel of the LORD spoke very solemnly to Jeshua and said, "This is what the LORD of Heaven's Armies says: If you follow my ways and carefully serve me, then you will be given authority over my Temple and its courtyards. I will let you walk among these others standing here." ~ Zechariah 3:4-7

You blind Pharisee! First wash the inside of the cup and the dish, and then the outside will become clean, too. ~ Matthew 23:26

Now repent of your sins and turn to God, so that your sins may be wiped away. ~ Acts 3:19

Don't you realize that those who do wrong will not inherit the Kingdom of God? Don't fool yourselves. Those who indulge in sexual sin, or who worship idols, or commit adultery, or are male prostitutes, or practice homosexuality, or are thieves, or greedy people, or drunkards, or are abusive, or cheat people—none of these will inherit the Kingdom of God. Some of you were once like that. But you were cleansed; you were made holy; you were made right with God by calling on the name of the Lord Jesus Christ and by the Spirit of our God. ~ 1 Corinthians 6:9-11

Because we have these promises, dear friends, let us cleanse ourselves from everything that can defile our body or spirit. And let us work toward complete holiness because we fear God. ~ 2 Corinthians 7:1

Do everything without complaining and arguing, 15 so that no one can criticize you. Live clean, innocent lives as children of God, shining like bright lights in a world full of crooked and perverse people. ~ Philippians 2:14-15

If you keep yourself pure, you will be a special utensil for honorable use. Your life will be clean, and you will be ready for the Master to use you for every good work. ~ 2 Timothy 2:21

You have had enough in the past of the evil things that godless people enjoy — their immorality and lust, their feasting and drunkenness and wild parties, and their terrible worship of idols. Of course, your former friends are surprised when you no longer plunge into the flood of wild and destructive things they do. So they slander you. But remember that they will have to face God, who will judge everyone, both the living and the dead. ~ 1 Peter 4:3-5

Blessed are those who wash their robes. They will be permitted to enter through the gates of the city and eat the fruit from the tree of life. ~ Revelations 22:14

Day 30

It all blew up today! My wife called it all off, asked me to bring her keys back and leave her alone for good. She accused me and my family of things that we would never do and have never done! I have confessed it all. I have admitted to all that I have done, what else can I do??? I can't be any more apologetic. I have done all I can to make things right. I have never blamed her and have taken responsibility for everything! So what else can I do? I KNOW I'VE BEEN CHANGED! So what's the matter now?

Now I understand why God and my therapist warned me about seeking acceptance and approval from others! I hear Him saying in the midst of this storm, "You are right where I want you." I don't feel like it, but I've got to trust you! I've been through too much; I have to trust you! I have nothing left to give or lose; I HAVE TO TRUST YOU!

So am I just trash now because of what I did in the past? Am I just supposed to be thrown away?? Is there no redeeming quality or value in me? Am I worthless because she doesn't want me anymore? THE DEVIL IS A LIE! Jesus died for me too! His blood covers my sins too!! I have been forgiven and redeemed too! I have repented, turned away, and stopped doing the things I used to do, so why is it STILL not good of enough for her? Because I'm doing it for her; ONLY WHAT I DO FOR CHRIST WILL LAST!

I brought the keys to her place and put them in her new car (on the way?) at the church that morning. (Yup! We bought her a new car!) In spite of the fact she chose to sit by her "friends" at "our" new church instead of with her husband, I was not angry and I didn't make a scene; that part of me is dead and gone, and I will not resurrect it because of this!

I have to admit; it hurt me to my bones when she walked into the church and sat down next to someone else rather than sit by her husband. That hurt! I wanted to get up and leave and never come back, but I didn't. I cried. I did; I cried like a baby silently right there in my seat, but oddly enough those tears washed the last of whatever was in me that had no business being there out of me. The last of my anger was washed away. The last of my fear of losing her was washed away. The last of my uncertainty of what God was going to do in me, for me, with me and through me was washed away. I was hurting, but knew somehow it was going to be okay. I didn't know how, I just know it would be.

I wasn't wrong this time; I had done all that God had asked me to do...this time. Now I was expecting God to do what He said He would do if I did what He told me to. For once in my life I was just going to believe Him in the middle of my worst pain. I literally said in my broken spirit, "Alright now, if you be God, then I need you to do what you promised." Somewhere in the middle of my silent tears and broken heart I heard and felt Him say, "You are right where I want you."

It was test time for me. Was I going to go back to the old me to put her in check, let her know that I didn't do anything and she had no right to embarrass me in church like that; or was I going to stand on what God had built up in me over the last 30 days??? Am I really changed or have I fooled myself? Is this the new real me or the same old fake one?? GOD, AM I READY FOR THIS? Once again, "You are right where I want you," is all I heard.

If I messed this up, I had a strong feeling it would be my last chance. I had to keep telling myself over and over again I was changed and right where God wanted me. I had to make myself believe that and not listen to the old me saying "leave" or "get her straight!"

I noticed the old me couldn't make up "its" mind, "Do I leave or get her?" Which one is it? I then realized that was the problem all along; the old me didn't know what to do. I was out of control going from one extreme to the other! Now I understood and could see clearly why I did some of the irrational things I had done:

walking away from an ex-wife who never did anything wrong to me or in our marriage; blaming everyone else for my mistakes and "their" inability to fix me; thinking everyone either did me wrong or would eventually; and not trusting, believing or surrendering to the very God that I preached about... The old me was unstable and had no idea what to do, so I did what I felt was "safe" instead of what was right. Well today was not the day! The old me finally showed himself to me as inadequate to protect, lead or guide my life any longer. I was going with the God-made new me even in the midst of my tears!

After the service ended, I wiped my face and asked the pastor if we could meet to discuss our marriage. My wife had not been willing to counsel on our marriage in quite some time, but I was determined and made my request known as the Word said. I walked out of that church shaking, wobbly, and unable to speak without crying, but I was walking! I was still standing! I had taken a major hit, but to God be the glory, I was still there! No one came to my aid, no one called to check on me from the church who had clearly seen that there was a problem, but God never left my side. He drove us home. He carried me upstairs. He got me out of my clothes. He put me to rest. He stayed right there! He never once reminded me of what I had done wrong, but He told me He was proud of me for what I did right! I had a Father who was pleased with me and was right there to tell me.

I was a little boy all over again before I was molested, before I was abused, before I became a liar, before I became angry, before I became promiscuous, before my mother died, before my marriages, before my divorces, before I had a child out of wedlock, before I had affairs, before I began to run from my problems, before I walked out on good people who loved me unconditionally, before I became a bad father, before I was diagnosed with cancer, before I filed bankruptcy, before my father died, before I became an abuser, before I lost my integrity and character, before I stepped down from my church. Before this marriage, separation, and pain... BEFORE IT ALL!

I was a little boy in my Father's arms safe and secure and I was okay for the first time in a long time!

God, I am finally right where you want me; I was Your child before I was anything else.

My Help for Day 30

But He *was* wounded for our transgressions, *He was* bruised for our iniquities; The chastisement for our peace *was* upon Him, And by His stripes we are healed. All we like sheep have gone astray; We have turned, every one, to his own way; And the LORD has laid on Him the iniquity of us all. He was oppressed and He was afflicted, Yet He opened not His mouth; He was led as a lamb to the slaughter, And as a sheep before its shearers is silent, So He opened not His mouth. ~ Isaiah 53:5-7

But the LORD was pleased to crush Him, putting Him to grief; if He would render Himself as a guilt offering, He will see His offspring, He will prolong His days, And the good pleasure of the LORD will prosper in His hand. ~ Isaiah 53:10

You are good and do only good; teach me your decrees. Arrogant people smear me with lies, but in truth I obey your commandments with all my heart. ~ Psalm 119:68-69

My suffering was good for me, for it taught me to pay attention to your decrees. Your instructions are more valuable to me than millions in gold and silver. ~ Psalm 119:71-72

But if any of you lacks wisdom, let him ask of God, who gives to all generously and without reproach, and it will be given to him. But he must ask in faith without any doubting, for the one who doubts is like the surf of the sea, driven and tossed by the wind. For that man ought not to expect that he will receive anything from the Lord, being a double-minded man, unstable in all his ways. ~ James 1:5-8

Draw near to God and He will draw near to you Cleanse your hands, you sinners; and purify your hearts, you double-minded. ~ James 4:8

"I am the Alpha and the Omega — the beginning and the end," says the Lord God. "I am the one who is, who always was, and who is still to come — the Almighty One." ~ Revelations 1:8

For the Lamb on the throne will be their Shepherd. He will lead them to springs of life-giving water. And God will wipe every tear from their eyes. ~ Revelations 7:17

I heard a loud shout from the throne, saying, "Look, God's home is now among his people! He will live with them, and they will be his people. God himself will be with them. He will wipe every tear from their eyes, and there will be no more death or sorrow or crying or pain. All these things are gone forever." ~ Revelations 21:3-4

And he also said, "It is finished! I am the Alpha and the Omega — the Beginning and the End. To all who are thirsty I will give freely from the springs of the water of life. ~ Revelations 21:6

The Final Days of Winter

I have not been able to write for a couple of weeks due to all that has been going on. It has been tough, but I am getting through my days and making it through my nights by the grace of God.

I was on a business trip to New Orleans the other day and I decided to drive through the neighborhoods destroyed by Hurricane Katrina before my meeting. I couldn't help but think about all that had happened recently: my wife came and got the last of her things and now her feeling is she never loved me and I had no idea what love was so we never should have been married!

Man! There are still houses with the markings on them indicating that someone died inside from the storm!

God, why is she treating me like this? She wants a divorce. "Her" pastor supports the divorce and has given her sermons series to prepare her for it and help her through it...

Man! There are streets that used to be main thoroughfares that are still blocked off due to the storm!

God, why was the pastor encouraging me to hang in there if she was counseling my wife to get out? *Note to self: If I ever get another chance to pastor, truly become the pastor I always wanted and needed most in a situation like this!*

When I asked her what scripture she was basing her support for a divorce on, she snapped and said, "What did Moses say!" She was standing on Deuteronomy 24:1... Her last words to me were, *"I am a wife; I'm just not your wife!"*

Man! How can an area that was once so full of life near downtown New Orleans still be dead after the storm?

God, why is she so angry and bitter? I called a meeting with the pastor. I was told that based on Deuteronomy 24:1, my wife was not only justified in divorcing me, but also no longer had an obligation to the marriage and I had brought this on us by the hardness of my heart and my unwillingness to change. Also that I had fell short as a pastor, husband and man because I slept with my wife before we got married, and I allowed her to live with me when she told me she was being put out of her home, so as a result the marriage was never honored by God and was doomed from the start. I was told if we had counseled with the pastor and her husband before we got married, we never would have been married... Wow! We didn't even know them then!

Man! Where was the help for all these people to restore and rebuild their homes, families and lives? Aren't their lives worth saving?

God, is there no redemption, salvation or forgiveness possible for a sinner like me? The devil is a liar! Now I understand why I had to go through all of this; I might have given up and killed myself out of shame if I simply believed what was being said about me and didn't know You for myself!

They finally asked my wife if there was anything in her at all that was willing to work on this marriage without any influence from anyone in her family. Her answer was *"Absolutely not!"* They asked me the same question. My answer was *"Most definitely!"* They said since she was not willing and I was, then there was nothing that they could do and we needed to settle our affairs right then and there. They also told us to stay away from each other so I don't do anything that would cause one of us to get hurt or end up in jail...

Man! Don't the people see that a change has taken place and new life is possible still in New Orleans?

I now know that I was not a bad person as they tried to imply, but a good person who made some bad choices. GOD, I KNOW THAT I'VE BEEN CHANGED! *Thank You for showing me I did not need the approval or acceptance from people. I have a personal, REAL relationship with You now!! You are my Shepherd I shall not want!!!*

The pastor asked how I was feeling now based on what was said, to which I answered, "I'm just going to accept what God allows." My wife got up and left. I left and never tried to call or bother her again. Ever...

I began to get extremely depressed looking at all that was lost in the hurricane; all the destruction caused; and all the death. I then began to cry to God about all the destruction I caused in my marriage and that deep down in my heart, I really didn't blame my wife for wanting to leave. The more I drove, the more damage and destruction I saw, the more depressed I became. I heard what my wife was saying loud and clear, "I'm a wife; I'm just not your wife! I never loved you and *never* should have married you! I don't want <u>YOU</u> anymore!"

The difference between the old me and the new me in Christ Jesus is the fact I love myself now and I know He loves me!!! While hearing, "I never loved you" hurts, knowing God will NEVER stop loving me heals!!!

I know that regardless of how she feels or what she does, I'm still her husband and I have to cover her with my best prayers to God the Father. I have to be willing to forgive her just as I have been forgiven. I still have to be priest, protector and provider; even more now than ever before! However, I have to do all of this without being with her, if she chooses not to be with me. God accepts her decisions, so I have to be willing and able to do the same.

I also have to honor our marriage whether she felt obligated to do so or not. I have to continue to wear my ring-I'm still married; I have to remain faithful-I'm still married; I can't let anyone else "comfort me"-I'm still married! I realized that my marriage vows finally meant more to me than how I felt, what I like or don't like; I am finally committed and married to God!

I told God that I felt like I had met my match. My wife was doing to me what I had done to others in the past and it hurt!

I heard God say quietly, "But you know what happens after you, right?" I had to think about it for a minute, then it hit me: everyone, after having been walked out on and given up on by me, had gone on to have awesome relationships! They survived! In fact, they prospered!

God said, "Now it's your turn." He said, "By the way, did you notice that everything the pastor said about you was past tense?" I wasn't that person any longer! I could feel God give me a holy hi-five!

I dried my tears up and turned the car around. I made a U-turn and started heading back towards downtown New Orleans. I was now leaving all of the destruction behind me and driving to the part of the city which had been rebuilt and looked brand spanking new!

Father, thank you for turning my situation around. I was praying for You to save my marriage and You had a plan to save my life! I'll stick with Your plan in the name of Jesus! AMEN!

<u>My Help for the Final Days of Winter</u>

So I am writing to you not because you don't know the truth but because you know the difference between truth and lies. ~ 1 John 2:21

So you must remain faithful to what you have been taught from the beginning. If you do, you will remain in fellowship with the Son and with the Father. And in this fellowship we enjoy the eternal life he promised us. ~ 1 John 2:24-25

I am writing these things to warn you about those who want to lead you astray. But you have received the Holy Spirit, and he lives within you, so you don't need anyone to teach you what is true. For the Spirit teaches you everything you need to know, and what he teaches is true—it is not a lie. So just as he has taught you, remain in fellowship with Christ. ~ 1 John 2:26-27

Then Jesus shouted, "Father, I entrust My spirit into Your hands!" And with those words He breathed His last. ~ Luke 23:46

And the one sitting on the throne said, "Look, I am making everything new!" And then he said to me, "Write this down, for what I tell you is trustworthy and true." ~ Revelations 21:5

And he also said, "It is finished! I am the Alpha and the Omega — the Beginning and the End. To all who are thirsty I will give freely from the springs of the water of life. ~ Revelations 21:6

All who are victorious will inherit all these blessings, and I will be their God, and they will be my children. ~ Revelations 21:7

We think you ought to know, dear brothers and sisters, about the trouble we went through in the province of Asia. We were crushed and overwhelmed beyond our ability to endure, and we thought we would never live through it. In fact, we expected to die. But as a result, we stopped relying on ourselves and learned to rely only on God, who raises the dead. ~ 2 Corinthians 1:8-9

A Change In Season

To every husband, wife, father, mother, brother, sister, son or daughter who may have received this by whatever means necessary, I simply, but with authority, say to you SEASONS CHANGE!!! You do not have to stay in the season that you're in! Change, however, starts with YOU!

Stop fighting with each other and start fighting for your change in season – the nchange in YOU!

THERE IS HELP...GET IT!!! Don't let your pride, your past or bad advice from others stop you from getting it or making you believe that help is not needed or going to work for you.

IT WILL! I touch, agree and believe it for you and your family. In fact, I declare it and decree it on your behalf in the name of Jesus, AMEN!

Help for the CHANGE IN SEASON

For Suicide, Immediate/Imminent Violence or Danger –
CALL 911 IMMEDIATELY!!!

Alcohol Issues:

Al-Anonymous/Alateen Family Group Headquarters

PO Box 862, Midtown Station

New York, NY 10115

800.356.9996

212.302.7240

National Council On Alcoholism & Drug Dependents Hope Hotline

800.622.2255

Child Related Issue:

American Association for Lost Children, Inc.

PO Box 41154

Houston, TX 77241

800.375.5683

713.466.1852

Child Abuse Prevention/Kids Peace Hotline

800.257.3223

Child Support Enforcement

800.622.KIDS (5437)

Children Rights/Youth Crisis Hotline

800.442.4673

Father Advocacy, Information & Referral Corp

(Helps fathers of children with custody, support, etc.)

800.722.FAIR (3247)

Federal Office of Child Support Enforcement

202.401.9370

National Youth Crisis Hotline

800.447.6263

Runaway Hotline

800.231.6946

Counseling/Psychotherapy

American Association of Christian Counselors

800.526.8673

Academy of Clinical Mental Health Counselors

National Board for Certified Counselors

800.398.5389

National Association of Social Workers

800.638.8799

Physical & Emotional Abuse:

AMEND

(Abusive Men Exploring New Direction)

303.220.1911

Batterers Anonymous

714.355.1100

Domestic Violence Hotline

800.96.ABUSE (22873)

Domestic Violence Information

800.FYI.CALL (394.2255)

Sexual Assault Recovery Anonymous

604.584.2626

<u>Drug Abuse:</u>

800-COCAINE

800.262.2463

National Institute of Drug Abuse

800.729.6686

Bible Scripture References

- The Amplified Bible Classic Edition (AMPC) Copyright © 2015 by The Lockman Foundation, La Habra, CA 90631

- Contemporary English Version® Copyright © 1995 American Bible Society

- Holman Christian Standard Bible® Copyright © 1999, 2000, 2002, 2003, 2009 by Holman Bible Publishers

- The King James Version (KJV) - Public Domain

- *The Message.* Copyright © 1993, 1994, 1995, 1996, 2000, 2001, 2002

- New King James Version® (NKJV®) Copyright © 1982 by Thomas Nelson

- New Living Translation copyright © 1996, 2004, 2007, 2013 by Tyndale House Foundation

-

About the Author:

Pastor André (AJ) Jones is saved by the grace of God. As a result, he is redeemed by the blood of the Lamb, restored and is energetic, spirit-filled and on fire for the Lord!

Passionate about ministry, he is committed to helping people believe that they can be forgiven, redeemed and restored from anything they may have done "BC" (Before Christ). Pastor Jones challenges them to truly develop a <u>real</u> relationship with Christ by teaching them the Word of God and how to use what they have in Him to deal with the challenges they face in their lives today. He is the Senior Pastor of the Cullen Missionary Baptist Church in Houston, TX which was founded by Bishop Robert C. Jefferson in 1977. He was also the Senior Pastor of the historic, 126 year old Spring Hill Baptist Church in Calvert, TX and the founder of the AMEN Fellowship Church on the campus of Texas Southern University.

In his "spare" time, Pastor AJ Jones is fulfilling a dream as a Sports Director for several gospel stations around the state & created a nationally syndicated Christian sports talk show called Faith In Sports.

He has also worked as a bank vice president, product manager & branch CFO over a 14-year career in corporate America.

Pastor AJ holds doctorate degrees in Theology and Divinity & has served in various positions in the Body of Christ:

- Assistant Pastor
- Youth Pastor
- Associate Minister
- Youth Leader
- Men's Ministry Leader
- Armor Bearer
- Founder of Church Youth Football
- Boys Rites of Passage Mentor
- Greeter

Pastor Jones is a humble servant and has been blessed to be used by God for ministry in churches, conferences, and workshops with emphasis on men, women, singles and youth all over the world. However, he is extremely motivated by the opportunity to make an impact on the Kingdom of God one life at a time.

Pastor AJ

www.ingramcontent.com/pod-product-compliance
Lightning Source LLC
Chambersburg PA
CBHW020851090426
42736CB00008B/337